Aristotle on Natural Simultaneity of Relatives in the *Categories*

This book addresses the issue of natural simultaneity of relatives, discussed by Aristotle in *Categories* 7, 7b15–8a12.

Natural simultaneity is a form of symmetrical ontological dependence that holds between items that are not causally linked. In this section of the *Categories*, Aristotle introduces this topic in his analysis of relatives and maintains that although relatives seem to be for the most part simultaneous by nature, there seem to be some exceptions. He mentions two pairs of relatives as exceptions, namely the pairs knowledge/knowable and perception/perceptible, and argues at length for the priority of the second relative over the first one in each case. Through a close reading of this text, the author analyses Aristotle's arguments for the thesis of the exceptional character of these pairs and shows that all of them are unsuccessful in supporting the thesis. In order to draw this conclusion, the author highlights and carefully considers the properties that Aristotle is committed to attributing to relatives, taking into account the metaphysical framework of the *Categories* as well as their specificities within the set of non-substantial categories. Then, he shows that Aristotle's mature views on relatives in the *Metaphysics* can be construed as committing him to the rejection of such a thesis.

Although the issue of natural simultaneity is just one of several that Aristotle considers in his discussion of relatives throughout *Categories* 7, it is a particularly relevant issue, since it involves a number of puzzles whose analysis allows for a better understanding of the very notion of relativity in Aristotle. This is the first book to explore this issue from the perspective of illuminating the Aristotelian views on relatives.

Aristotle on Natural Simultaneity of Relatives in the Categories will appeal to scholars and graduate students working on Aristotle, ancient philosophy in general, and metaphysics.

António Pedro Mesquita is Professor at the Department of Philosophy and member of the HPhil Research Group of the Centre of Philosophy of the University of Lisbon. He recently co-edited (with Ricardo Santos) the book *New Essays on Aristotle's Organon* (Routledge, 2023).

Routledge Focus on Philosophy

Routledge Focus on Philosophy is an exciting and innovative new series, capturing and disseminating some of the best and most exciting new research in philosophy in short book form. Peer reviewed and at a maximum of fifty thousand words shorter than the typical research monograph, *Routledge Focus on Philosophy* titles are available in both ebook and print on demand format. Tackling big topics in a digestible format the series opens up important philosophical research for a wider audience, and as such is invaluable reading for the scholar, researcher and student seeking to keep their finger on the pulse of the discipline. The series also reflects the growing interdisciplinarity within philosophy and will be of interest to those in related disciplines across the humanities and social sciences.

The Virtue of Playfulness
Why Happy People are Playful
boomer trujillo

Moral Blackmail
Coercion, Responsibility, and Global Justice
Ben Colburn

Aristotle on Natural Simultaneity of Relatives in the *Categories*
António Pedro Mesquita

For more information about this series, please visit: www.routledge.com/Routledge-Focus-on-Philosophy/book-series/RFP

Aristotle on Natural Simultaneity of Relatives in the *Categories*

António Pedro Mesquita

First published 2025
by Routledge
605 Third Avenue, New York, NY 10158

and by Routledge
4 Park Square, Milton Park, Abingdon, Oxon, OX14 4RN

Routledge is an imprint of the Taylor & Francis Group, an informa business

ISBN: 978-1-032-90095-7 (hbk)
ISBN: 978-1-032-91428-2 (pbk)
ISBN: 978-1-003-56326-6 (ebk)

DOI: 10.4324/9781003563266

Contents

Acknowledgements

This monograph has benefited from the useful commentary and criticisms of audiences on several occasions in which parts of it were presented, namely in Madrid, São Paulo (twice, first in an online conference and then in an in-person seminar), Catania, Ouro Preto, and Curitiba. I am especially thankful to Roberto Bolzani, Tomás Calvo†, Fernando Gazoni, Lorenzo Giovannetti, Owen Goldin, Victor Gonçalves, Evan Keeling, Fabio Morales, Manuel Oliveira, Guilherme Riscali, Ricardo Santos, Eduardo Wolf, and Marco Zingano. A number of clarifications as well as some of the objections that I address throughout the text resulted, at least in part, from their commentaries. I am indebted to Matt Duncombe for his careful reading of a full draft of the book and his incisive comments on the text, as well as his encouragement to publish it. I am also very grateful to the anonymous readers who commented on earlier versions of the manuscript and whose insightful remarks helped me to correct, clarify, develop, and improve several points in my argument. Needless to say that all the remaining mistakes are my own. Finally, I would like to deeply thank Evan Keeling for his help with the English text.

The final form of this monograph was prepared during a stay as a visiting professor at the University of São Paulo (USP), which was only possible thanks to the sabbatical leave granted to me by my school, the School of Arts and Humanities of the University of Lisbon (FLUL), the support of the São Paulo Research Foundation (FAPESP) and the generous hosting of the Faculty of Philosophy, Letters and

Human Sciences of USP. I would like to express my deepest thanks to these three institutions.

This work was funded by Portuguese national funds through FCT – Fundação para a Ciência e a Tecnologia, I.P., within the project PTDC/FER-FIL/0305/2021.

Abbreviations

Aristotle's Works

APo.	*Posterior Analytics*
Cat.	*Categories*
De an.	*On the Soul*
EN	*Nicomachean Ethics*
GA	*Generation of Animals*
IA	*Progression of Animals*
Int.	*De interpretatione*
Juv.	*On Youth and Old Age*
Metaph.	*Metaphysics*
Mete.	*Meteorology*
PA	*Parts of Animals*
Ph.	*Physics*
SE	*Sophistical Refutations*
Sens.	*Sense and Sensibilia*
SomnVig.	*On Sleep*
Top.	*Topics*

Plato's Dialogues

Chrmd.	*Charmides*
Euthd.	*Euthydemus*
Prm.	*Parmenides*
R.	*Republic*
Sph.	*Sophist*
Tht.	*Theaetetus*

Ancient Commentaries

All ancient commentaries will be referred to by the general conventional abbreviation *In Cat.*, with the exception of the three following works:

Introd.	Sergius of Reshaina's *Introduction to Aristotle and his Categories*
Prol.	Olympiodorus' *Prolegomena*
Scholia	Anonymous scholia to the *Categories*

1 Introduction

1.1 Overview

From time to time, Aristotelian readership welcomes a new paper (more rarely, a new book) on relativity in Aristotle.[1] It is apparently not the hottest of topics, considering the (relatively) modest overall number of studies devoted to it over the past 60 years or so; but it is indeed a tenacious one. As the titles in the note show, recent years have seen a somewhat unusual accumulation of contributions on the subject. I propose to add to it as well, from a specific point of view, namely the natural simultaneity of relatives discussed by Aristotle in *Cat.* 7, 7b15–8a12.

This issue has been inexplicably neglected by modern commentary.[2] This is unfortunate though, for the analysis that Aristotle offers there involves more than a few puzzles. I will here mainly focus on one of them, concerning the special status that Aristotle reserves in his analysis for two pairs of relatives, namely knowledge/ knowable and perception/perceptible, to which I will refer in what follows as the "problematic pairs".[3] As we will shortly see, a number of other puzzles will join us along the path.

In this text, Aristotle maintains that, although relatives seem to be for the most part simultaneous by nature, there seem to be some exceptions; he mentions those two pairs as exceptions and argues at length for the priority of the second relative over the first one in each case. In this book, I will evaluate the arguments he puts forth in support of the thesis of the exceptional character of the problematic pairs in this regard and, as a consequence, the soundness of the thesis itself, and conclude that neither in isolation nor taken together

DOI: 10.4324/9781003563266-1

do these arguments succeed in proving the thesis, which should therefore be rejected.

Before I do that, however, an effort of conceptual clarification has to be made about the key notions involved, namely the very notion of relatives and the notions of simultaneity and natural simultaneity. Accordingly, the structure of this book is the following: first, I will consider and discuss some aspects of the notion of relatives in Aristotle (Chapter 2); then, I will examine in detail the notion of natural simultaneity within the general notion of simultaneity and how it applies to relatives (Chapter 3); finally, I will present Aristotle's position on the natural simultaneity of relatives, analyse and discuss the arguments he advances for the exceptional character of the problematic pairs, and, consequently, assess his thesis in this regard (Chapter 4). I will then try to unravel the train of thought that led Aristotle to profess this thesis in the *Categories* and show how his mature views on relatives in the *Metaphysics* may be seen to commit him to the rejection of it, and therefore to confirm that he has evolved from the former treatise to the latter in regard to the specific point of the natural simultaneity of relatives (Chapter 5).

I deem the exercise in clarification and analysis thus undertaken valuable in itself, insofar as it puts on the table a topic of Aristotelian reflection that has been rather overlooked (and unjustifiably so) by modern commentary. However, I think it is especially valuable because the solution to the puzzles involved in such a topic provides us the means for a better understanding of the very notion of relativity in Aristotle.

That said, let me begin by putting all of this in context by sketching Aristotle's approach to relatives throughout Chapter 7 of the *Categories*. In my sketch, I will understandably give more room to the issues that will play a part in the discussion of my point than to those that will not, and therefore I will inevitably disregard many otherwise important matters, namely some of those that have mainly attracted the eye of modern commentators.

1.2 The Context

As in Chapter 5, on substance (2a11–19), and again in Chapter 8, on quality (8b25), Chapter 7 begins with a general characterisation of the items that fall under the category studied in the chapter, in this case, relatives. This characterisation is as follows:

> We call relatives all such things as are said to be just what they are *of* or *than* other things, or in some other way *in relation to* something else.[4]

This characterisation, illustrated and clarified by the subsequent analysis, gives us two relevant pieces of information about relatives: the first is that every relative has a correlative; the second is that what makes something a relative is *to be said to be just what it is* in relation to its correlative. For example, something is said to be *larger* in relation to something *smaller*, which is its correlative, and it is in relation to this that it is said to be just what it is, namely larger; the same holds, for example, for double and half. All relativity is therefore constituted within some correlativity, and always involves a pair of items.[5]

Let us set down the rule underlying this notion, which I will call the "rule of the correlativity of relatives" (RC), as follows:

> *RC = Every relative has a correlative, in relation to which it is said to be what it is.*

Next in the text comes the presentation of several groups of examples of relatives, among them the ones just mentioned (6a37–b14). The nature, content, organisation, and succession of these groups is certainly relevant from a philosophical point of view, but not directly to the point in question; so, as in all similar situations, for reasons of economy, I will not pay attention to it here.

Following the model already applied in the two previous chapters, regarding substance and quantity, the characteristics of relatives are then discussed. The first two, the admission of contrariety (6b15–19) and the admission of a more and a less (6b19–27), are not distinctive properties (ἴδια) of relatives, in the technical sense, since, although there are relatives that satisfy them, not all do.[6] This is, however, the case with the following characteristic, namely the fact that relatives are said in relation to a correlative that reciprocates (πρὸς ἀντιστρέφοντα λέγεται), which is shared by *all* relatives and – it can reasonably be assumed – *only* by relatives.[7] It is curious, however, that, in this case, Aristotle does not expressly say so, contrary to what he had done at the analogous junctures of his discussion of substance and quantity, and to what he will do again in the case of quality.[8]

This universal and exclusive feature of relatives expands upon the one contained in the initial definition, inasmuch as it adds to the point expressed in it that every relative has a correlative (in relation to which it is said to be just what it is) the *new* point that the latter, in turn, is said to be just what it is in relation to the former. What is characteristic of all relatives (and apparently only of them) is, therefore, the fact that they *reciprocate*, i.e., that the constitutive relation of a relative to its correlative is necessarily paired with the reciprocal relation (what we would now call their converse relation) of the latter to the former. So, if *x* is the double of *y*, *y* is the half of *x*; if *x* is master of *y*, *y* is slave of *x*; etc. In general, if a relative *x* is relative to a correlative *y*, *y*, in turn, is relative to *x* and has it therefore as its correlative.

As we did with the rule of correlativity of relatives, let us set down the rule of reciprocity of relatives (RR) as follows:

> *RR = If a relative is said to be R of its correlative, the latter is said to be R' of the former (R' being the reciprocal relation of R).*

Aristotle will then devote a substantial part of the discussion of this topic to presenting, framing, and resolving apparent failures of reciprocity of relatives (6b36–7a22). These failures are, according to him, of two types. In the first place, there are failures of reciprocity that seem to occur when "a mistake is made and that in relation to which something is said is not properly rendered" (6b36–38), as when we say that the wing is of a bird, instead of saying, as we should, that the wing is of a winged (thing); for it is qua winged, and not qua bird, that what has a wing has a wing (6b38–7a3). In cases such as these, the solution, he says, consists, as in the example just given, in properly rendering the correlatives (7a3–5). A second type of reciprocity failure seems to occur "if no name exists in relation to which a thing would be properly rendered" and it becomes necessary "to invent names" (7a5–7), as in the cases of the neologism "ruddered" to express the correct correlative of a rudder (since it is not insofar as it is said of anything else, for example, a boat, that a rudder is *of this*, but insofar as *this* simply has a rudder), or of the neologism "headed" to express the correct correlative of a head (for it is not insofar as, for example, it is an animal that a head is *of* that animal, but only insofar as that animal has a head) (7a7–18).[9] The solution in these cases consists, once again following the examples, in coining names "derived from the original relatives" and assigning them "to their reciprocating correlatives" (7a18–22).

This discussion then allows Aristotle to reiterate the initial statement ("all relatives, then, are said in relation to correlatives that reciprocate, provided they are properly rendered": 7a22–23) and to draw some inferences as to how to ensure that the reciprocity of relatives is always made clear (7a22–b14). The first inference is, quite understandably, the necessity to properly express the exact correlative of each relative (7a23–28) – for example, to say that a slave is slave of a master, instead of saying that he is slave of a man (7a28–31), even though this last statement is, of course, also true.[10] The second inference that Aristotle draws follows the first and is, in fact, a general methodological recommendation about the way to proceed so that it is always possible to adequately express the exact correlative of each relative, namely to abstract away all aspects that are accidental to the correlation, such as, in the case of the previous example, the fact that the master is a man, or a biped, or a being capable of knowledge (7a31–b1). The consequences of not following this recommendation will be, he says, that reciprocity, and with it the relativity of the relative, will not be made clear (7b1–9).

The discussion concludes with the following summary (7b10–14):

> One must therefore give as correlative whatever it is properly said in relation to. If a name already exists, it is easy to give this, but if it does not, it may be necessary to invent a name. When correlatives are given thus, it is clear that all relatives will be said in relation to correlatives that reciprocate.

We arrive thus at our main point. As a fourth trait – one, again, apparently not distinctive of relatives[11] – Aristotle mentions natural simultaneity. In his own words, "relatives seem to be simultaneous by nature, and in most cases this is true" (7b15–16). He then gives examples of relatives that, in his view, are simultaneous by nature, namely the pairs double/half and master/slave, which he justifies as follows: pairs like these are simultaneous by nature, because, within each pair, when one of the relatives exists, the other also exists, and when one of them is missing, the other is also missing (7b16–22).[12] However, according to him, there are also pairs of relatives that do not seem to satisfy this condition of natural simultaneity. The examples he gives are, in the order they appear, the pair knowledge/knowable (7b23–35) and the pair perception/perceptible (7b35–8a12). To support his position in the first case, he presents three arguments (at 7b24–27, 7b27–33 and 7b33–35); and, to support it in the second, he presents two arguments (at 7b36–8a6 and 8a6–12). I will later on devote a substantial part of this book to the detailed analysis of each of these arguments.[13]

Here ends the point concerning natural simultaneity. We now enter the last part of the text – the one that has attracted by far the greatest interest on the part of modern commentators – in which Aristotle raises a difficulty (8a13–28) and proposes a solution to it (8a28–b21). The difficulty consists in knowing "whether no substance is called a relative, as it seems, or whether this is possible with regard to some secondary substances" (8a13–15). The solution proposed by Aristotle involves a reformulation of the definition of relatives given at the beginning. In the new, reformulated definition, relatives are now defined as "those things for which being is the same as being somehow related to something".[14] Indeed, according to him, this reformulation allows one, by means of what Sedley termed the "principle of cognitive symmetry",[15] to expel all substances from the relatives, namely the potentially problematic ones, that is, the parts of secondary substances (things like *the* head or *the* hand), and therefore to confirm that "no substance is a relative" (8b21).

There has been much discussion since antiquity about the status and content of this new definition and, most especially, about its relation to the one given in 6a36–37. I will avoid this discussion here, as it has no impact on the issue I want to address.[16] I must however say a few words about how I take the relation between the two definitions to be conceived and intended by Aristotle. As far as the text itself allows us to conclude, the new, reformulated definition is designed to clarify the notion of relatives with a view to solve a problem concerning its *extension*. This exercise in clarification serves the purpose of blocking certain items that would be admitted as relatives under the original definition, namely the parts of secondary substances, from being admitted as such; it does *not* serve the purpose of drawing distinctions between types of relatives, about which Aristotle has nothing to say in this section of the chapter. That is why the explicit conclusion of the section solely consists in making it official that, if the reasoning leading to it is sound, substances and relatives form two disjoint sets, no reference being made to specific members of the set of relatives or to any subsets it may contain. To be sure, nothing prevents one from drawing consequences regarding the latter issues from such a line of reasoning; and maybe someone actually came to do so – for instance, the Stoics, if Simplicius' testimony on their views on relativity is accurate[17] and historical research could trace them back to the reading of this section of the *Categories*. What seems to lack any basis, considering the actual text, is to ascribe such consequences to Aristotle himself. So, the bottom line is that, quite frankly, I fail to see any textual grounds for interpretations according to which the two definitions offered in *Cat.* 7 somehow correspond to different types of relatives or two different degrees of relativity.[18] One final word to say that, be it as it may, it seems safe to assert that the validity of RC and RR is not affected by the new definition of relatives. Not only does nothing in the text suggest otherwise, but the point of variation between the two accounts does not concern the satisfaction of any of these rules. Moreover, at least RC seems to be as easily deducible from the second one as it is from the first, even if one must adopt a specific wording in each case.[19]

In a rather atypical way, which clearly contrasts with the end of the remaining chapters dedicated to the categories, chapter 7 closes on a sceptical note, with what seems to be a statement of retrospective reservations about the analysis carried out (8b21–24):

> It is perhaps hard to make firm statements on such questions without having examined them many times. Still, to have gone through the very difficulties is not unprofitable.

It is inevitable to ask about the scope of these observations: do they apply only to the point just discussed, namely the possibility of certain substances being relatives, or to the entire analysis developed throughout the chapter? In antiquity, most commentators leaned towards the first interpretation.[20] Today, the second interpretation is more common.[21] I (undogmatically) share the latter reading, as it seems to me more in line with the tentative and hesitant nature of the whole discussion developed in this chapter.[22]

1.3 The Problem

It is against this backdrop that the issue of natural simultaneity of relatives must be analysed. As we have seen, Aristotle states, when beginning the discussion of this issue (7b15–16), that relatives appear to be simultaneous by nature (ἅμα τῇ φύσει) and that in most cases this is true. Evidently, the first question that must be answered before proceeding is what is to be understood by "natural simultaneity". The answer does not seem difficult, since, in the *Categories* themselves, in the final section known as the "postpredicaments", a chapter is dedicated to the notion of simultaneity (Ch. 13), which immediately follows another devoted to the notion of priority, in line with which it should be seen. Now, by consulting these chapters, it becomes clear that Aristotle seems to be using the second sense of simultaneity, defined in Chapter 13, 14b27–33, shortly after having introduced and defined the one he describes as the "unqualified and strictest" sense of simultaneity, namely temporal simultaneity (14b24–26).

According to this second sense of simultaneity, things that satisfy both of two conditions are simultaneous by nature: (1) they must reciprocate as to implication of existence; and (2) neither of them can be the cause of the other's existence. And "to reciprocate as to implication of existence" (ἀντιστρέφειν κατὰ τὴν τοῦ εἶναι ἀκολούθησιν) means, in Aristotle's idiolect, that, if one of the simultaneous things exists, the other also exists, and if one ceases to exist, the other also ceases to exist.[23] Hence, simultaneous *by nature* are those things that reciprocate as to implication of existence, in this sense, without it being the case that either is the cause of the other's existence.

A strong indication that this is the sense that is already at work in the notion of natural simultaneity used in *Cat.* 7 is the fact that, after giving examples in which, according to him, the natural simultaneity of relatives is verified, Aristotle confirms their simultaneity with the fact that the existence of either one of them entails the existence of the other and the "destruction" of any one of them entails the "destruction" of the other, which, as we have just seen, corresponds exactly to the notion of reciprocation as to implication of existence in the sense introduced in *Cat.* 13. Additionally, the example of natural simultaneity Aristotle gives in Chapter 13 is the simultaneity between double and half (14b29–33), which was also one of the examples of relatives given in chapter 7 to justify why "in most cases it is true" that relatives are simultaneous by nature (7b16–22).[24]

Examples of relatives that, according to Aristotle, are in fact simultaneous by nature are, as we have also seen, the pair double/half and the pair master/slave (7b16–18). However, he adds that it does not appear to be true that all relatives are simultaneous by nature (οὐκ ἐπὶ πάντων δὲ τῶν πρός τι ἀληθὲς δοκεῖ τὸ ἅμα τῇ φύσει εἶναι: 7b22–23), since the knowable seems to be prior to knowledge (τὸ γὰρ ἐπιστητὸν τῆς ἐπιστήμης πρότερον ἂν δόξειεν εἶναι: 7b23–24) and the perceptible seems to be prior to perception (τὸ γὰρ αἰσθητὸν πρότερον τῆς αἰσθήσεως δοκεῖ εἶναι: 7b36). Thus, the relatives that, for reasons that he then sets forth in detail, do not seem to him to satisfy the condition of natural simultaneity are the pairs knowledge/knowable and perception/perceptible, both of which are examples of relatives that he had already mentioned at the beginning of the chapter, following the presentation of the first definition of relatives (at 6b2–6) and which belong to the core group of relatives in the various lists that Aristotle offers, both in the *Categories* and outside of it.[25]

A pertinent question that could be asked here is why Aristotle hastens to say that the relatives seem to be simultaneous by nature, even adding that this is true *in most cases* (ἐπὶ τῶν πλείστων), only to later end up saying that, nevertheless, this is not the case for *all* relatives. Perhaps it could be conjectured that his intention was to eliminate natural simultaneity as a candidate for being another ἴδιον of relatives, reserving this status only for reciprocity, stated immediately before, at 6b28–7b14. This conjecture makes sense, but it is vulnerable to the following objection. Aristotle considers that all opposites are naturally simultaneous.[26] Now, since there are opposites in other categories besides relatives, namely in that of quality, even if all relatives were naturally simultaneous, other things that are not relatives would *also* be naturally simultaneous, so that, for this reason, natural simultaneity could never be a distinctive property of relatives.[27] From this perspective, Aristotle would not need to invoke any failures of natural simultaneity of relatives to maintain that this is not an ἴδιον of relatives, since that would be a given from the start. However, there is, perhaps, a reply to this objection, namely to conceive opposites as being naturally simultaneous in *another* sense of natural simultaneity, distinct from the aforementioned. And the fact is that, as we will see later,[28] Aristotle also gives the name of "natural simultaneity" to a third sense of simultaneity, which concerns the coordinated species of the same genus. In saying in those two passages from the *Topics* that opposites are naturally simultaneous, it may be that Aristotle had in mind a sense analogous to the latter, or at least inspired by it and developed from it, and not the sense relevant to the relatives.[29] In this case, Aristotle's concern, in *Cat.* 7, to eliminate natural simultaneity as a potential alternate ἴδιον of relatives would be justified.

This, however, is not the problem we need to focus on. The problem we need to focus on is rather the following. That certain relatives *are not* simultaneous by nature, in the sense described above, does not seem to me to raise any doubts. Obvious counterexamples are all relatives that are causally related to their correlatives. Indeed, in this case, even if the two relatives reciprocate as to implication of existence, they will not be naturally simultaneous according to that sense of natural simultaneity. A paradigmatic example would be that of the parent/child pair, in which the two relatives reciprocate as to implication of existence, but one of them is the cause of the other's existence. Thus, it would have been easy for Aristotle to use this example, or another equivalent one, and, with it, to find the exception he needed to prove that, although most relatives are simultaneous by nature, this is not true in all cases, namely if his intention was really to eliminate natural simultaneity as a candidate for an ἴδιον of relatives. This is not, however, what he does, but instead he presents as examples of failures of natural simultaneity the relatives knowledge/knowable and perception/perceptible. Yet, the question that can be asked is whether specifically these two pairs of relatives *should be considered non-simultaneous by nature*, considering, in particular, the arguments that Aristotle puts forward for this. Indeed, it is not clear, for instance, whether, in his treatment of these two problematic pairs, Aristotle is fully respecting the rules to which he is bound by his own analysis of relatives, namely the rules concerning the proper rendering of correlatives, or if the arguments advanced by him for the exceptionality of those pairs with regard to natural simultaneity actually lead to this conclusion.

As we shall have occasion to see in some detail later, a large number of influential ancient commentators, and some modern ones, have disputed Aristotle's claim that not all relatives are simultaneous by nature, and have even asserted that, on the contrary, natural simultaneity is a distinctive property of relatives.[30] However, if we take into account the notion of natural simultaneity that we have described, this seems to be simply wrong. As we have seen, all relatives that are causally related to their correlatives are not, for that very reason, naturally simultaneous. Therefore, Aristotle is right in what he says at 7a15–16: not all relatives are simultaneous by nature; therefore, natural simultaneity *is not* a distinctive property of relatives. The problem is that it is not on the basis of this claim that he maintains that not all relatives are simultaneous by nature, but on the basis of an analysis of some relatives that apparently *are not* causally related, namely the two problematic pairs referred to. Which legitimately raises the question whether, besides being right about the thesis, Aristotle is also right *in the analysis*. The point, differently put, is therefore: it seems safe to say that Aristotle is right that not all relatives are simultaneous by nature (and hence that the ancient and modern authors mentioned are not); but is he also right *for the reasons* he gives for it?

Considering these reasons and the theoretical context to which Aristotle is committed, the short answer is "no". I will dedicate the rest of this book to the long answer. To support this answer, I will use the following methodology. Firstly, I will begin by discussing some aspects of the notion of relatives in Aristotle and fix the nomenclature that I will use to refer to them from then on. Next, I will analyse in detail the notion of natural simultaneity and how it applies to relatives. Finally, I will present Aristotle's position on the natural simultaneity of relatives, reconstruct, examine and evaluate the arguments he proposes in favour of the exceptional character of the problematic pairs, and, as a consequence, assess the thesis defended by him in this regard.

Notes

1 Apart from the commentaries and notes inserted in translations of the *Categories* and the *Metaphysics* into several modern languages, see: Perinetti 1956; Philippe 1958; Cavarnos 1975; Caujolle-Zaslawsky 1980; Conti 1983; Sillitti 1985; Mignucci 1986; Morales 1994; Demetracopoulos 1996; Palù 2000; Sedley 2002; Hood 2004; Jansen 2006; Rini 2010; Bonelli 2011; Harari 2011; Zucca 2011; Crubellier 2013; Ebbesen *et al.* 2013; Gambra 2013; Gourinat 2013; Luna 2013; Duncombe 2015; Brower 2016; Erismann 2016; Marmodoro/Yates 2016; Martin 2016; Bonelli 2018; Duncombe 2018; Duncombe 2020; Moon 2021.

2 Compare particularly to the double account of relatives in that chapter, by far the most commented issue in the last few decades. A recent exception is Edelhoff 2020, whose monograph is consecrated to the analysis of natural priority in the *Categories*, and which, therefore, gives detailed attention to the issue of natural simultaneity of relatives (one of the book's four chapters is devoted to this issue).

3 These two pairs can be included in a larger class that has recently been called (originally by Hood 2004: 56, following sporadic similar usage in previous literature) "intentional relatives" – a designation which is, I think, self-explanatory. Although I assume it is safe to guess that Aristotle would allow the conclusions he draws about them to apply to the whole class, I will restrict myself to considering the said pairs when commenting on the text of *Cat.* 7. I will however have something to say about the class as such later on (see below, Chapter 5).

4 Πρός τι δὲ τὰ τοιαῦτα λέγεται, ὅσα αὐτὰ ἅπερ ἐστὶν ἑτέρων εἶναι λέγεται ἢ ὁπωσοῦν ἄλλως πρὸς ἕτερον (6a36–37). (I use Minio-Paluello's text.

All translations of the *Categories* are Ackrill's, with occasional minor adaptations.) The Neoplatonic commentators avoided using the term "definition" for this characterisation, as well as for the one that Aristotle will propose later, at 8a31–32, preferring, since Porphyry, to present them as "descriptions" (ὑπογραφαί); Porphyry's argument (*In Cat.* 111.17–20 Busse) is that the categories, being supreme genera, admit of no definition. However, it is Aristotle himself who refers to it as a definition (ὁρισμός) at 8a29 and 8a33. The Platonic ancestry of this characterisation of relatives seems evident; see, for example, *Republic* 439a1–2 and *Sophist* 255c13–14. According to Simplicius (*In Cat.* 159.12–15 Kalbfleisch), this was already remarked in antiquity, namely by Boethus of Sidon (fr. 25 Rashed). But the point divided Neoplatonic commentary: Porphyry (*In Cat.* 111.27–29 Busse) admits, although without expressly taking a position, that the first definition (and specifically its first part) goes back to Plato, being followed by Boethius (*In Cat.* 217c Migne); Olympiodorus (*In Cat.* 112.19–23 Busse) and Elias (*In Cat.* 205.20–21 and 215.21–22 Busse) attribute it entirely to Plato, as does the anonymous Syriac catechetical commentary (§ 18 Aydin); as for Ammonius (*In Cat.* 70.10–14 Busse), Philoponus (*In Cat.* 109.26–28 Busse) and Simplicius (*In Cat.* 159.15–22 Kalbfleisch; but cf. 162.36 and 163.6–11), they all reject (the first two vigorously) that it is Plato's. Sergius of Reshaina limits himself to saying (repeatedly) that the definition was given by people "who were before him" or that it was "provided by the ancients" (*In Cat.* 320, 324, 325, 343, 349 Arzhanov). A similar characterisation of relatives occurs again in *Cat.* 10, 11b24–33, and 12b16–25 (and cf., by way of anticipation, *Cat.* 6, 5b11–6a11), as well as in *Metaph.* V 15, 1021a26–30.

5 Aristotle seems to ignore or at least disregard here relations that involve more than two relatives, as well as reflexive relations, although he would probably deal with the latter as he does with the notion of δύναμις in *Metaph.* V 12, 1019a15–16, when he describes it as "a principle of movement or change in another thing *or in a thing qua other*". A passage on sameness in *Metaph.* V 9, 1018a7–9, provides grounds for this hypothesis. Note that, outside of his official treatment of the relatives in the *Categories* and *Metaphysics* V, a few passages in the *corpus* seem to imply that Aristotle acknowledges relations involving more than two relatives as well: see especially *Topics* IV 4, 125a14–22 (and see, in the same direction, Morales 1994: 270n31 and Hood 2004: 18–19).

6 Remember that, for Aristotle, a *distinctive property* "is that which does not exhibit the essence of a thing, but belongs only to it and counterpredicates with it" (ἴδιον δ' ἐστὶν ὃ μὴ δηλοῖ μὲν τὸ τί ἦν εἶναι, μόνῳ δ' ὑπάρχει καὶ ἀντικατηγορεῖται τοῦ πράγματος: *Top.* I 5, 102a18–19, Brunschwig's text). It seems rather agreed upon that it is in this technical sense that Aristotle uses the notion of ἴδιον in his analysis of categories in *Cat.* 5–8.

7 The first statement is made repeatedly throughout the chapter (6b28, 7a22–23, 7b10–14) and also outside of it, namely in *Cat.* 10, 12b21–22, and *Top.* VI 12, 149b12.

8 Cf., respectively: 5, 4a10–11; 6, 6a26–27; 8, 11a15–19. Most Neoplatonic commentators (with the notable exception of Ammonius) consider that this feature of relatives is their ἴδιον: see Porphyry, *In Cat.* 115.17–18 Busse; Philoponus, *In Cat.* 113.13–14 Busse; Simplicius, *In Cat.* 179.27–180.1 Kalbfleisch. In modern times, this interpretation was vigorously challenged by Caujolle-Zaslawsky 1980: 176–181.

9 These two examples, like others of the same kind, will later on be dismissed by Aristotle as not being true relatives (cf. 8a28–b21), but this does not affect the point he is making here.

10 Bodéüs 2001: 123n2 justifiably draws attention to the fact that, in the chapter on relatives in *Metaphysics* V, the distinction between properly expressed and inappropriately expressed correlativity is formulated in terms of the pair καθ' αὑτό vs. κατὰ συμβεβηκός: applying the example of the text, when a certain man is master of a slave, the master is a relative *per se*, while the man is a relative *per accidens* (*Metaph.* V 15, 1021b3–11). It should perhaps be added that the omission of any reference to this conceptual pair is all the more salient here considering that earlier, in 6, 5a38–b10, Aristotle had underlined an analogous distinction between per se quantities, that is, quantities proper, and accidental quantities, namely entities which, not being themselves quantities, nevertheless have a certain quantity.

11 As we shall see, this claim was disputed in antiquity as it is still disputed today.

12 "For double and half are simultaneous, and if there is a half there is a double, and if there is a slave there is a master; and similarly with the others. Also, one carries the other to destruction; for if there is not a double there is not a half, and if there is not a half there is not a double. So too with other such cases." (Ἅμα γὰρ διπλάσιόν τέ ἐστι καὶ ἥμισυ, καὶ ἡμίσεος ὄντος διπλάσιόν ἐστιν, καὶ δούλου ὄντος δεσπότης ἐστίν· ὁμοίως δὲ τούτοις καὶ τὰ ἄλλα. καὶ συναναιρεῖ δὲ ταῦτα ἄλληλα· μὴ γὰρ ὄντος διπλασίου οὐκ ἔστιν ἥμισυ, καὶ ἡμίσεος μὴ ὄντος οὐκ ἔστι διπλάσιον· ὡσαύτως δὲ καὶ ἐπὶ τῶν ἄλλων ὅσα τοιαῦτα.) As is well known, classical Greek does not have a specialised verb for existence and uses instead the verb "to be", as is here the case. However, "existence" is as much a πολλαχῶς λεγόμενον as "being" is. So, this begs the question of how the co-existence of these pairs of relatives should be understood here and in the parallel occurrences within the *Categories*. Let us keep in mind this question, which I will address when the appropriate time comes, namely, when discussing the notion of natural simultaneity (see below, Chapter 3.3., *ad fin.*).

13 See below, Chapter 4.

14 Οἷς τὸ εἶναι ταὐτόν ἐστι τῷ πρός τί πως ἔχειν (8a32). This reformulated definition also appears in *Top.* VI 4, 142a22–33, and VI 8, 146a36–b9; but see *SE* 31, 181b25–37, and *Metaph.* XIV 1, 1088a21–b4.

15 Sedley 2002: 327.

16 Among the proposed interpretations, I highlight as particularly useful those by Caujolle-Zaslawsky 1980, Mignucci 1986, and, above all, those by Sedley 2002 and Duncombe 2015 (integrated as chapter 6 of Duncombe 2020).

17 See *In Cat.* 166.15–29 Kalbfleisch.

18 As Sedley 2002, the most eminent and influential representative of this line of interpretation, puts it. Sedley himself sees the limits of his interpretation in 338–339 and 345.

19 The point of RC under the second account consisting in making it explicit that the very being of a relative consists in being related to a correlative. However, for the purposes of our discussion, there is no reason to abandon the original formula.

20 See, for example, Porphyry (*In Cat.* 126.24–32 Busse), Ammonius (*In Cat.* 80.9–13 Busse), Philoponus (*In Cat.* 132.23–133.4 Busse), and Simplicius (*In Cat.* 200.34–201.10 Kalbfleisch).

21 Cf. Caujolle-Zaslawsky 1980: 176; Oehler 1984: 252; Zanatta 1989: 598; Zucca 2011: 193, 211n23; Gambra 2013: 227. Moon 2021: 469 is a recent exception: he thinks that Aristotle's final reservations apply specifically to the immediately preceding discussion and, in particular, to the issue of the categorial status of parts of substances such as heads and hands; but see also Sedley 2002: 338–339.

22 A sign of this is the prevalence of the expression δοκεῖ ("it seems that") and other cognate expressions throughout the chapter.

23 The first conditional is explicitly stated at 13, 14b30–31 (and cf. the equivalent notion of priority, i.e., not to reciprocate as to implication of existence, at 12, 14a29–35). The second is not, but it can be deduced from the first, by contraposition. For, let *x* and *y* be two items that reciprocate as to implication of existence. Then, according to the explicit statement in 14b30–31, if either of them exists, the other exists as well. From this it follows that, if *x* exists, *y* exists, and therefore, by contraposition, that, if *y* does not exist, *x* does not exist; and again that, if *y* exists, *x* exists, and thus, by contraposition, that, if *x* does not exist, *y* does not exist.

24 Of course, one may object that Aristotle could be using here a simpler notion of natural simultaneity, a notion that is reduced to the first condition required in *Cat.* 13 – maybe one of Platonic origin, wholly congenial to the notion of priority whose use he attributes to Plato in *Metaph.* V 11, 1019a1–4. But I fail to see how this could be the case unless the postpredicaments were a late addition to the *Categories*, if not a post-Aristotelian one; and the burden of proof that this is indeed the case would then be entirely on the objector. In line with the interpretation I favour, Caston 2018 (see

39–40n8) and Edelhoff 2020 (see 34, 39–41) have recently argued that, in his analysis of natural simultaneity in *Cat.* 7, Aristotle is already using the complete, double-condition notion offered in *Cat.* 13 (and, in a somewhat similar vein, see Duncombe 2020: 108–109). In any case, as we shall see, the very interpretation of the notion of natural simultaneity in the sense discussed in the text and of the scope of its application raises difficulties, which I will consider and discuss later (see, below, chapter 3).

25 See, for knowledge/knowable (sometimes one member of the pair remains implicit): *Cat.* 7, 6b2–6; 6b15–16; 6b34–35; 7b23–31; 8, 11a24–36; 10, 11b27–31; *Top.* II 8, 114a18–19; IV 1, 121a1; IV 4, 124b19; VI 6, 145a14–15; VI 8, 146b1–2; VI 8, 146b5; VI 8, 146b6–8; VI 12, 149b11; *SE* 31, 181b34–35; *Metaph.* V 15, 1020b32; 1021a29–30; 1021b6; X 6, 1057a7–12; 1057a16. And, less ostentatiously, for perception/perceptible, see: *Cat.* 7, 6b2–6; 6b35–36; 7b35–8a12; *Top.* II 8, 114a19; *Metaph.* V 15, 1020b31. These two pairs already occur as examples of relatives in Plato: see, for instance, *Chrmd.* 165c–166e and 167d–168e; *R.* 438ce; *Tht.* 156ac; *Prm.* 133c–134e.

26 Cf. *Top.* V 3, 131a12–20, and VI 4, 142a22–24.

27 This was noted in antiquity by some authors whom Simplicius refers to but does not name (*In Cat.* 194.28–195.16 Kalbfleisch), and whose position he later seeks to reject in a not particularly persuasive way (195.16–30). Note that one could also draw a symmetrical conclusion from those two texts of the *Topics* and, with it, raise a serious problem for the thesis defended by Aristotle regarding natural simultaneity of relatives. Since, according to *Cat.* 10, 11b17–33, relatives are opposites, if all opposites are simultaneous by nature, so must *all* relatives be. But it would perhaps be possible to argue that, when Aristotle speaks of opposites in those two passages, he is specifically thinking of contraries and contradictories, considering, therefore, a kind of restricted sense of opposition, which encompasses only these two types, as happens, for example, in *Ph.* V 3, 227a8–9.

28 See Chapter 3.1, below.

29 Note that, if so, this would also solve the problem referred to above, in note 27.

30 Among ancient commentators see: Porphyry, *In Cat.* 117.32–35 and 119.4–6 Busse; Ammonius, *In Cat.* 76.10–77.2 Busse; Philoponus, *In Cat.* 117.4–5 Busse; Simplicius, *In Cat.* 189.19 Kalbfleisch (for whom this is, moreover, "the main distinctive property of relatives": τὸ μάλιστα ἴδιον τῶν πρός τι); Olympiodorus, *In Cat.* 108.17–109.19 Busse; Elias, *In Cat.* 213.17–26 Busse; Sergius of Reshaina, *In Cat.* 334–342 Arzhanov and *Introd.* § 75 Aydin. The beginning of Simplicius' commentary on this point indicates that this interpretation can be traced back to Pseudo-Archytas (see *In Cat.* 189.19–31). Furthermore, some of those authors even consider that Aristotle, despite his literal words in the chapter, accepts that natural simultaneity is an ἴδιον of relatives: this is the case of Porphyry

(119.4–6), Olympiodorus (108.22–109.12), Elias (214.27–215.11) and Sergius of Reshaina (*In Cat.* 334–342; *Introd.* §75). (Simplicius seems more hesitant in this regard: see, on the one hand, 189.27–29, and, on the other hand, 183.13–14, 190.31–33 and 193.33–194.19.) In a somewhat opposite sense, but in an equally suggestive way, we are told by several sources that some ancient authors, whose names they do not disclose, defended that the *Categories* were spurious, on the grounds, inter alia, that the author of this treatise considered that some relatives do not satisfy the condition of natural simultaneity, contrary to what would be, according to them, Aristotle's authorised position: see, for instance, Olympiodorus (*Prol.* 22.38–24.20 Busse) and the anonymous scholiast to the *Categories* (*Scholia* 33a28–b34 Brandis); there are still echoes of this tradition in the Arabic reception (cf. Georr 1948: 152–153). Significant exceptions to this dominant interpretation are Boethius (*In Cat.* 233bd Migne) and Averroes (*Middle Commentary* §59). Among modern commentators, a recent example along the lines of this interpretation, although of course with a different formulation, is Duncombe 2020: 110–112.

2 Relatives

2.1 Aristotle's Views on Relatives

What sorts of things are the relatives for Aristotle? In recent literature, there has been some discussion of this question. An important part of the motivation behind this discussion is the concern to distinguish the relatives from the substances they put in relation, without thereby reducing them to the relations themselves, which, as is well known, Aristotle only very exceptionally and always only derivatively acknowledges.[1]

The solution I adopt simply results from a comparison of relatives with items in other "secondary" categories, that is, non-substantial ones:

(1) Let us assume that Socrates is good and that the mountain over there is beautiful. What are the qualities in these two cases? Paronymically expressed, the qualities are *good* (the being good of Socrates) and *beautiful* (the being beautiful of the mountain).
(2) Let us assume that Socrates is 1.70 metres tall and that the mountain over there is 2000 metres high. What are the quantities in these two cases? The quantities are *1.70 metres* (Socrates' being 1.70 metres tall) and *2000 metres* (the mountain's being 2000 metres high).
(3) Socrates is, as we know, the son of Sophroniscus; and let us admit that that mountain is greater than this one. What are the relatives in these two cases? The relatives are *son* (Socrates' being a son in relation to Sophroniscus) and *greater* (that mountain's being greater in relation to this one).

DOI: 10.4324/9781003563266-2

The moral of the story is that there is no more risk of confusion between substances and relatives than there is (or rather, there is not) between substances and qualities or quantities. Relatives, like qualities or quantities, have modes of being that are independent of the substances in which they inhere, despite the fact that they themselves are always ultimately dependent on them. Like qualities and quantities, relatives are *properties* of a subject, with which they should not be confused, despite the fact that, by being affected by such properties, the subject can be truly said to be qualified, quantified, or related to something in a certain way.[2] At the same time, on this interpretation, relatives are not reduced to relations, nor are the latter seen as in any way prior and/or superior to the former.[3]

Bearing this in mind, I will henceforth distinguish between, on the one hand, the relative and correlative *properties*, and, on the other hand, the relatum and the correlate put into a relation by them, which are the *subjects* affected by these properties. A relatum and its correlate are whatever items that are affected by converse relational properties, and insofar as they are affected by them; the relative and the correlative are the properties in virtue of which the former are so affected. Accordingly, I will observe in a technical way the nomenclature that serves this distinction, that is, "relative" and "correlative" for the properties, and "relatum" and "correlate" for the subjects that are affected by these properties.[4] Of course, inasmuch as they are affected by relational properties and put into a mutual relation by them, the subjects themselves may be said to be *relatives* to one another from that particular point of view and spoken of as *relative things*, without any violation of the rule that has just been set.

2.2 Relatives and the Ontological Square (I)

Let us now consider a difficult issue that arises from a specificity of relatives, which is unparalleled in any other category. The specificity is that relatives, as we have seen, always come in pairs; and, further, that, as stated in 6b28–7b14, all relatives reciprocate, which entails that, if a certain x is R of a certain y, then y is R' of x (R' being the reciprocal, or converse, relation of R).

Let us then assume that someone eats half a cake and leaves the other half.[5] How should we conceive the correlation the subsisting half has with the double, which no longer exists? Should it be said that the correlation was interrupted and also ceased to exist as soon as one of the relatives ceased to exist? If so, this does not seem to correspond to our linguistic habits, nor, therefore, to what one would intuitively expect. Isn't it common, and acceptable, to say something like "I only have half the cake left"? Now, in the very terms of Aristotle's analysis, isn't saying that only half of the cake is left over an improper, colloquial way of saying that half *of the double* is left? Hence, if we value these linguistic habits (as, in equivalent circumstances, Aristotle usually does), it seems that, despite the disappearance of the double, the half/double correlation remains; and, if the half/double correlation remains, then, by the principle of reciprocity, the double/half correlation remains as well. But how, if there is no longer any double?

The difficulty increases if we remember that relatives are accidents and that, in terms of the doctrine set out in *Cat.* 2 – which, for simplicity's sake, I will call from now on the "doctrine of the ontological square" – all accidents inhere in a subject (or "are in a subject").[6] Let us consider now, then, the case of a son whose father has died, or a master whose slave was killed. Again, ingrained linguistic habits, which are prima facie justified, allow statements such as: "My father died"; or: "They killed my slave" (let us remember the *Euthyphro*). Thus, if, here too, we value these linguistic habits, we will have to admit that the father/child and master/slave correlations are maintained. But, by the same reasoning, if the child is the child of the father, the father, by reciprocity, is the father of the child; and, if the master is the master of the slave, the slave is the slave of the master. Now, in the cases described, in which subject does the relative-father inhere, and in which subject does the relative-slave inhere?[7]

Let us consider a particular case. Sophroniscus is the father of Socrates and, reciprocally, Socrates is the son of Sophroniscus. Thus, being the son of Sophroniscus is an accident that inheres in Socrates and being the father of Socrates is an accident that inheres in Sophroniscus. But what happens when Sophroniscus dies? It seems reasonable to say that when he dies, Socrates remains his son;[8] and, apparently, without a problem, because the accident being-son-of-Sophroniscus continues to inhere in Socrates. But, since being-son-of reciprocates with being-father-of, *where does the accident being-father-of-Socrates inhere from the moment Sophroniscus died*?

Obviously, this difficulty becomes particularly acute if, as Aristotle maintains is the case for the pairs knowledge/knowable and perception/perceptible, the two relatives are not naturally simultaneous, but one of them is prior to the other, such that the former can exist without the latter, but not the latter without the former. In fact, such a situation seems to blatantly contradict the doctrine of the ontological square. For if a thing *x* is *already* knowable by some knowledge *K* that does not yet exist, it seems that there are, after all, relatives without correlatives, since to the relative-knowable there corresponds, in this case, no correlative. However, the initial characterisation of relatives (and, incidentally, also its reformulated version), reinforced by the universal rule of reciprocity, establishes that this is impossible. Assume, then, alternatively, that the knowability of thing *x*, already existing, has a correlative; and that this is prospective knowledge *K*, which does not yet exist. Then, this knowability is an accident of the thing *x* and inheres in it; but in what does the said prospective knowledge inhere, in the entire time when knowledge *K* does not exist? The very terms of the question attest to the absurdity that an answer in these terms would involve. However, even if one accepts that a relative and its correlative may not be naturally simultaneous, one thing that, for the reasons given above, cannot be accepted is that they do not reciprocate. Therefore, if a certain knowability inheres in a certain subject, its correlative must also inhere in some subject.

2.3 Relatives and the Ontological Square (II)

The point is obviously important and, despite the fact that a more thorough discussion could benefit from a deeper analysis of the notion of simultaneity in Aristotle as well as his position regarding the failure of simultaneity of the two problematic pairs, we can, for now, consider and try to solve the difficulties exposed, in a general way.

The first difficulty mentioned, that of half and double, perhaps admits a simple solution. Simplicius, using another example, suggests the following:

> For even if he is called a father after the death of his son, *he is so-called by reference to the time when [the son] was alive.*[9]

In other words, adapting this to our example: we can continue to speak of the half of a double that no longer exists, because we do so with reference to the time when it still existed. The half/double correlation remains as something that can be referred to even after there is no longer a double, because there was a time when there was; and the same, of course, holds in all analogous cases.[10]

The second difficulty, concerning what subjects relatives whose relata have ceased to exist inhere in, is, however, much thornier. Porphyry seems to be aware of this difficulty and, although he does not explicitly recognise it, at a certain point develops an interpretation of relatives that would perhaps allow him to resolve it. He says:

> Relatives are present in their subjects neither as essential complements of them nor as any sort of accident that comes to be in their subject, as for example an affection or an activity, *but they are external to their subjects*. It is for this reason that they can come to be and pass away without their subjects being affected.[11]

In fact, this point of view, if it could be shared by Aristotle, might help to explain how a relative can subsist as such after its correlative has ceased to have a subject of inherence (e.g., a son maintaining his filiation relationship after the substance-father has died), namely because of the alleged inter-independence, as it were, of relatives and their subjects. The problem is precisely whether Aristotle could share this point of view. I am strongly inclined to conclude that he could not, since the exceptionality that Porphyry attributes in this passage to relatives within the set of non-substantial beings does not seem to have any support in the doctrine of the ontological square, which governs the ontology underlying the whole theoretical discussion developed in the *Categories* and with which, therefore, all of it must be in harmony.[12]

A tempting solution to the second difficulty would be to think that, in cases such as those considered, a single relatum is sufficient to support correlativity: a kind of "love for the both of us". Thus, in cases such as these, the relative-father and the relative-slave would not have any subject of inherence, but they would not need one either, because the relation would be entirely supported by the subsisting relata, the substance-child and the substance-master, respectively, "by reference to the time" when the correlated substances existed. But this does not appear to be how Aristotle thinks of the matter, and the solution does not seem compatible with the central thesis of the *Categories* (entirely in harmony with the principles of the ontological square, from which it is deduced) according to which everything that is not a primary substance is either in a primary substance or is said of a primary substance.[13] Indeed, if the master/slave correlation holds, both relatives hold; and, given the specific nature of this correlation, since neither of them is a primary substance, *both* must be in, or be said of, a primary substance, which precisely, in the circumstances under consideration, is not the case, because one of them is *neither* in a primary substance *nor* is it said of a primary substance.

Yet is it really true that, in this kind of case, one of the relatives is neither in a primary substance nor is it said of a primary substance? Granted that one of them is not *in* a primary substance; couldn't it still be the case that it is *said of* a primary substance? For, let us assume that relatives are universal accidents that are predicated of individual subjects; for instance, that the relative-father is a universal that is predicated of Sophroniscus, Socrates, Callias, and many other individuals. Then, when Sophroniscus is already dead and Socrates is still alive, although there is no subject of inherence for the relative-father in this particular correlation, one could say that there is, in a way, a subject of predication. In fact, precisely insofar as it remains true to say that, in that situation, Sophroniscus is the father of Socrates, the relative-father is *now* said of a primary substance, albeit of a primary substance that no longer exists. Hence, relatives are said of primary substances after all, and therefore the conformance with the requirements of the doctrine of the ontological square seems duly preserved.

Could this be an appropriate solution for our current predicament? I think not. First of all, let us remind ourselves that, in terms of the standard reading of the ontological square (a reading that goes back to Porphyry and the whole Neoplatonic interpretation), universal accidents correspond to the third type of being described in the ontological square and these are defined by both being said of a subject and *being in* a subject.[14] Now, if this is so, even if relatives are universal accidents that are said of primary substances, *they still must have subjects of inherence*. Here we go again, then: for, what would be the subjects of inherence in cases such as these?

There is however a stronger objection than this one. Let us, for the sake of the argument, call "universal accidents" the third type of being described in the ontological square, as we have done just now, and, continuing to follow the traditional reading of the ontological square, call "particular accidents" the second type of being (regardless of the metaphysical nature we wish to ascribe them). According to that reading, as we saw, universal accidents are those that are both said of a subject and in a subject, and particular accidents are those that are in a subject but are not said of a subject. Whichever interpretation of the particular accidents one favours, either as individuals or as themselves universals, though maximally determined,[15] it is, I think, rather uncontroversial that they fall under universal accidents and are predicated by them: the particular pallor of Socrates falls under the universal Pallor, which (let us assume) falls under the broader universal White, which in turn falls under the broader universal Colour, and so on; and for that reason the pallor of Socrates is a colour. Now, from this it follows that each time a universal accident is *said of* a primary substance a particular accident under the former is *in* that substance. The reason for this is, quite simply, that you can only truly say of a primary substance that it is *P* if it is true that some *P-ness* is found in it. If it is true that Socrates is pale (which is short for "if it is true to say of Socrates that he is pale", or, again, "if it is true that paleness is said of Socrates"), then some particular pallor is in him; differently put, if no particular pallor is in Socrates, then it is not at all true that Socrates is pale. The corollary of this is that it cannot be the case that something is *said of* a primary substance without something being *in* that substance. In general, if a universal accident is said of a primary substance, then a particular accident is in that substance. Therefore, if we simply assume that relatives are universal accidents that are said of individual subjects and that there are such accidents in the world, we must assume something further, namely that there also are relatives which are particular accidents (either individuals or maximally determined universals) that are *in* these individual subjects.[16]

The bearing of this on our predicament is apparent: plainly put, to assume that relatives are universal accidents that are predicated of individual subjects is not a way out of it, since this assumption does not preclude, but instead entails, that, if any such accidents are predicated of these subjects, then particular relational accidents *inhere* in them; and therefore we are once again faced with the original problem, namely that, in cases such as the described, it is not clear what would be those subjects of inherence and, more basically, how there could be any.

So, whether or not we accept the line of reasoning we have been following, we are forced to look for a fuller and better solution elsewhere.

2.4 Temporally Asymmetrical Relations

A bold hypothesis would be to admit that, at least in the case of relatives, and for only one in each pair, the reference to the primary substance required by the aforementioned thesis of *Cat.* 5 for all things that are not primary substances could be made in times that are deferred from those in which these latter exist. In other words, to admit that, specifically in these cases, the inherence of the relative in relation to a subject could have occurred in the past (or, perhaps also, will occur in the future) and, thus, that it suffices that there had been (or, perhaps also, that there will come to be) a primary substance as the subject of the inherence. This would turn out to be a densification of the solution inspired by Simplicius. One could then say that, in the case of the master whose slave was killed, the correlation is maintained, because the relative inheres in a substance that exists now, while the correlative inheres in a substance that existed before; and the same applies, mutatis mutandis, in the case of the child whose father has died. One could give this special type of relation the generic name of "temporally asymmetrical relation". In temporally asymmetrical relations, the two relata exist in partially different times, but the relation itself (and, therefore, the correlativity and the reciprocity), if not stopped in the meantime, subsists for as long as any of them currently exists from the moment the relation was established.[17]

It is obviously hard to ascertain how much of this hypothesis could be credited to Aristotle himself and how aware he might have been of its explanatory power to fully integrate the relatives within the doctrine of the ontological square. The fact remains, however, that it is not otherwise easy to see how to accommodate, within the framework of that doctrine, situations such as those described, if one wants to preserve the intuitions that certain relations persist after one of the correlates ceases to exist. More to the point, it is a telling detail that the very case of the problematic pairs seems to show that Aristotle is more than willing to accept relations that are in place before one of the correlates *begins* to exist – relations for which an explanation within the framework of the ontological square must be supplied.

Now, if we accept this solution and let it apply to the future as well, this will also allow us to advance a little with regard to the situation of these pairs. Indeed, according to this solution, something of which there is currently no knowledge by which it would be knowable could nonetheless *already* be knowable, provided that there be someone capable of knowing it in the future. Note that, taking into account the principles to which Aristotle is committed by virtue of the doctrine of the ontological square, the condition must be read thus: provided not only that there *could* be someone capable of knowing it in the future, but that there actually *will be* someone capable of knowing it. Thus, the correlative of the knowable would not be mere potential knowledge, but rather potential knowledge *of an actual* subject of knowledge. To be sure, if that were the case, it would not always be possible, in cases like these, to determine *now* that something is knowable – and therefore to determine now that this something is a relative; but nothing would prevent its *being* so already.

Admittedly, this may seem odd at first. However, as Aristotle would put it, in the end one would find it odder if it would be otherwise. Let me argue that this is indeed the case here by showing how this interpretative hypothesis can be deductively linked to some basic, structural principles to which Aristotle is committed in the *Categories*.

Consider the following argument:

1: Relatives are not substances. [*Cat.* 4]
2: Everything that is not a primary substance is either in a primary substance or said of a primary substance. [*Cat.* 5, 2a34–b9]
3: Relatives must either be in a primary substance or said of a primary substance. [1, 2]
4: For every relative *r* there is another relative *r'* in relation to which it is said to be just what it is. [RC]
5: Relatives *r* and *r'* are correlatives to each other. [Definition of correlative]
6: Relatives and their correlatives must be both either in a primary substance or said of a primary substance. [3, 4, 5]

If the argument is sound, as it seems to be, it follows from the conclusion either that two correlatives must always be in a primary substance or said of a primary substance at all the same times, or that given two relatives that are correlatives to each other, if they are both neither in a primary substance nor said of a primary substance at some point in time, they must be in or said of a primary substance *at different points in time*. Now, intuitions that relations may persist after one of the correlates ceases to exist favour the second alternative; and Aristotle's treatment of the problematic pairs prima facie requires it. Hence, the existence of temporally asymmetrical relations as defined earlier follows from the conclusion of the argument and must therefore be acknowledged, if the argument is indeed sound.

Now, the argument clearly relies on 1, 2, and 4, which are Aristotelian principles, stated in the *Categories*. I fail to see how 1 and 2 could be seriously challenged. But neither does 4 seem to be easily dismissible. Not only does it correspond to RC, a rule that is deducible from *both* definitions of relatives in *Cat.* 7, but, if it were to be dismissed, how could one make sense of Aristotle's statement that, when it comes to the problematic pairs, one relative is prior *to the other*? If Aristotle wanted to deal with these pairs by cancelling RC, he would have just said that the problematic pairs simply aren't pairs, that they represent an exception to this rule, or are maybe even a counterargument to its validity, since, in these cases, relatives have not correlatives. However, this is not what we see him doing. What we see him doing is to advocate the priority of one *of the correlatives* over the other: which means that he views these pairs as failures of natural simultaneity of correlatives, not as exceptions to the rule of correlativity itself.

Considering what has been just said, and bearing especially in mind the theoretical constrains of the doctrine of the ontological square, I will therefore adopt this interpretative hypothesis as the one that best reconciles the categorial specificities of the relatives with that doctrine, and, in this sense, as being necessitated, and justified, by the consistence of the whole system.[18]

Notes

1 As it happens in *Metaph.* V 15, 1021b6–8, where Aristotle recognises as also being per se relatives "those things with reference to which their possessors are said to be relative" (καθ' ὅσα τὰ ἔχοντα λέγεται πρός τι: Reeve's translation), such as equality and similarity. Commenting on this passage, Bonelli 2011: 180 says, quite pertinently, that the relations appear in it *subordinated* to relatives (and cf. also Morales 1994: 256n2). However, for modern revaluations of relations in Aristotle in the opposite direction to the one assumed in the text, see Cavarnos 1975: 43–46, 63–65, and especially Hood 2004. In recent times, the discussion referred to in the text was initiated by Mignucci 1986.

2 This interpretation ends up coinciding with the one defended, with different arguments, by Mignucci 1986: 101–104. Duncombe 2020 has recently taken a stand against it. For him relatives are *the things themselves* insofar as they are constituted by a relation to something (see, for example, 97: "relatives are things that are constituted by a relationship to some correlative"; and 100: "a relative is an object that relates to something"); but it is not entirely clear to me how he understands this thesis (which, by the way, comes from Duncombe 2018: 122, 124–125), since he cannot, of course, mean that relatives are the substances themselves. Duncombe's interpretation was recently followed by Edelhoff 2020: 33,

n65, 35 and 38 (but see also Cohen 2008: 14–15 and Cohen 2013: 238). One more word of clarification: it should be noted that the subjects whose relatives are properties do not all have to be substances; for example, the subjects of double and half are quantities, and those of lighter and darker are qualities (for this last example, see *Ph.* V 1, 224b34–35). However, in terms of the metaphysical views that Aristotle expounds in the *Categories*, everything that is not substance, and, in particular, everything that is not a primary substance, must ultimately be in a primary substance or be said of a primary substance (cf. *Cat.* 5, 2a34–b9); and this includes those quantities and qualities which, from certain points of view, can be said to be relative to others, so that, ultimately, they themselves, and the relatives which have them as subjects, depend on substances.

3 From what is said in the paragraph it does not of course follow that there cannot be uncertainty and controversy over exactly in which category to place certain classes of entities, as Aristotle discusses with regard to the parts of secondary substances in 8a13–b21.

4 I follow here Morales 1994: 256n1 and Zucca 2011: 199n3.

5 This example is inspired by Bodéüs 2001: 125n3.

6 The designation "ontological square" was coined by Ignacio Angelelli in Angelelli 1967: 12–15. The author returned to this issue in Angelelli 1985. I will here use the expression "doctrine of the ontological square" both for the principles stated in *Cat.* 2 and for the consequences that Aristotle will draw from them later in the treatise, namely the very important one set forth in *Cat.* 5, 2a34–35, which I have already referred to above (note 2) and will shortly come back to. One further remark on terminology. As is well known, Aristotle does not use in the *Categories* the word συμβεβηκός or any of its cognates to refer to accidents – a concept which, in fact, is not explicitly mobilised throughout the treatise. However, it has been widely accepted since the time of the ancient Greek commentators that everything that is in a subject, in the terms set out in *Cat.* 2, does indeed correspond to what Aristotle calls "accidents" in other (and arguably later) works. In the same vein, I will therefore use this word as a convenient term for all the non-substantial entities listed in Chapter 4.

7 Erismann 2016: 420 evokes this problem with regard to the relationship between model and image, in cases where the latter persists, but the former has already disappeared. His observation is prompted by a particularly suggestive situation: certain iconophile Byzantine intellectuals of the eighth and nineth centuries argued that the image and its prototype are relative, in the Aristotelian sense of the term, and, at the same time, simultaneous by nature, including, for some of them, specifically those cases in which the prototype has long disappeared, e.g., Jesus Christ, the Virgin Mary, the apostles and the saints. Erismann sees clearly that this raises a problem: "The criterion of simultaneity of relatives implies the inherence

of an accidental relational property being-the-model-of. This property, like every accidental property, needs a bearer, an individual substance which is its substrate."

8 Plotinus was well aware of this: see *Enneads* VI.1.7.38–41. On this particular point he was not followed by most later Neoplatonic commentary: see, above all, Simplicius, *In Cat.* 190.5–30 Kalbfleisch, and Boethius, *In Cat.* 228bc Migne.

9 *In Cat* 190.16–18 Kalbfleisch, Fleet's translation; italics mine.

10 Note, however, that the conclusion that Simplicius himself intends to draw is not this, but the opposite: "Co-existing has two senses: to co-exist substantially is one thing, as light co-exists with the sun; to co-exist in terms of relationship, which does not always have essential reality equally; for when the son dies, the father loses his relational co-existence, since neither the son nor the father exist when the son is no more; for even if he is called a father after the death of his son, he is so-called by reference to the time when [the son] was alive." (*In Cat.* 190.12–17 Kalbfleisch, Fleet's translation.)

11 *In Cat.* 125.25–28 Busse, Strange's translation; my italics.

12 Simplicius also seems to be aware of this problem, when he admits, in the following terms, the subsistence of some relatives beyond the disappearance of their subjects: "Of relationships those which are joined essentially to their subjects co-exist with them, such as 'on the right' and 'on the left' in the parts of an animal; other relationships abandon their subjects although they persist, as 'on the right' in terms of standing, when it no longer fits the participation in the relationship (and these relationships are rather [to be considered as] accidental); *others endure although the subject passes away, as that of things that formerly existed*, and that of what is later to what is earlier in time *because relationships have incorporeal accounts* [λόγους] *in and for themselves*." (*In Cat.* 175.4–11 Kalbfleisch, Fleet's translation; my italics.) Clearly, the explanation that Simplicius puts forward is even further from Aristotle's theoretical universe than Porphyry's was: in addition to incorporating the (typically Plotinian) segregation of relations from relatives and the Platonising subordination of these to the former, he seems to be committed to the Stoic notion of λόγοι σπερματικοί (for this latter aspect, see Fleet 2002: 165n117). For these reasons, he could hardly provide us with any support here.

13 Cf. *Cat.* 5, 2a34–35 (and the subsequent lines up to b9).

14 The standard reading consists in rendering the four types of being that Aristotle distinguishes in *Cat.* 2 the following way: beings that are said of a subject but are not in a subject (1a20–21) are universal substances; beings that are in a subject but are not said of a subject (1a23–24) are particular accidents; beings that are said of a subject and are in a subject (1a29–b1) are universal accidents; beings that are neither in a subject nor said of a

subject (1b3–4) are particular substances. See: Porphyry, *In Cat.* 73.4–74.24 Busse; and cf. Ammonius, *In Cat.* 25.5–26.24 Busse; Philoponus, *In Cat.* 28.1–31.26 Busse; Simplicius, *In Cat.* 44.1–51.4 Kalbfleisch; and Boethius, *In Cat.* 169b–177a Migne.

15 I am of course referring, in general, schematic terms, to the so-called "traditional interpretation", supported by Jones 1949 and Ackrill 1963, among many others, both before and after these publications, and the revisionist interpretation originally proposed by Owen 1965, also followed by many adherents and opponents, respectively.

16 This is obviously in no way something specific to relatives, but something common to all accidents. However, for some reason, it seems more often overlooked in the case of relatives. We may therefore draw the general principle that to every universal accident that is predicated of a primary substance there corresponds a particular accident that inheres in that substance. A side, though relevant, remark relating to this is that, regardless of their metaphysical status, be it individual or universal, particular accidents, inasmuch as they inhere in individual subjects, are accidents *of* those subjects and, as such, peculiar to them; no matter whether the exact same shade of pale can be found in Erastus or in Coriscus, Socrates' pallor is, as such, Socrates' pallor and no one else's. Again, the same thing can of course be said of relatives, and this is not without consequences for some points I will have to make later.

17 One could ask how this type of relation should be seen in light of two passages where Aristotle considers inter alia the truth-value of present-tense declarative sentences about subjects that no longer exist, like "Homer is a poet" or "Socrates is ill". These are, respectively, *Int.* 11, 21a21–33, and *Cat.* 10, 13b12–35 – the former passage being usually seen as being somewhat at odds with the latter. Without entering into the details of these two texts, and especially of their mutual relation, I think it would be safe to say that they are both consistent with the notion of temporally asymmetrical relations. When Socrates is still alive, but his father Sophroniscus has already died, you can say that Sophroniscus is the father of Socrates by predicating the "is" in "an accidental way" and without therefore predicating it of Sophroniscus per se (meaning: without thereby assuming that Sophroniscus exists). But of course the rationale for you saying that Sophroniscus is the father of Socrates when Sophroniscus no longer exists is the fact that he once did; and therefore, in a proper grammatical sense, it is not true to say that Sophroniscus *is* the father of Socrates, but only that he *was* the father of Socrates. On the contrary, Socrates, who still is in the proper sense of the verb inflection, can be truly said to be now the son of Sophroniscus. The two subjects of inherence no longer coexist, but the relation exists, and therefore the two relatives do too, as they will as long as one of the relata will.

18 In addition, the explanation inspired by Simplicius maintains its validity in cases where neither of the two correlates exists. In these cases, the relation does not exist either; it is, however, admissible to speak of the relatives by reference to the past time when it did, that is to say, by reference to the past time when there was at least one of the relata: that is how one keeps talking of Socrates as a son of Sophroniscus long after they are both dead. The same, of course, does not apply to the future, for the very reason that the future is not set, and it is therefore undetermined which primary substances will come to exist. One may, of course, talk about *possible* relations, relata and relatives in the future, but that is an entirely different matter (as evidenced by the fact that one may also talk about possible relations in the past).

3 Natural Simultaneity

3.1 Simultaneity and Natural Simultaneity

Let us now turn, for a more thorough inspection, to the notion of simultaneity and, in particular, to the notion of natural simultaneity, in the sense relevant to the characterisation of relatives.

We have already seen that this notion plausibly corresponds to the second sense of simultaneity presented by Aristotle in chapter 13 of the *Categories* (14b27–33). This second sense is, in turn, built upon (and, in a way, in opposition to) two senses of priority presented in the previous chapter: the second sense, according to which things that do not reciprocate as to implication of existence in relation to others are said to be prior (no qualification added) to them (14a29–35); and the fifth, according to which things that *do* reciprocate as to implication of existence in relation to others, but are somehow the cause of their existence, are said to be prior *by nature* to them (14b10–23). The presentation of the different senses of priority is thus developed in chapter 12 – in a way that is far from being unparalleled in Aristotle[1] – in two moments: first, only four senses of priority are officially announced (14a26: πρότερον ἕτερον ἑτέρου λέγεται τετραχῶς), which are then presented in succession (14a26–b8); at the end, a fifth is unexpectedly added, which corrects and completes the previous list.[2] The reasoning that leads to this fifth sense is particularly suggestive: among prior things, there are those that do not reciprocate as to implication of existence in relation to others; however, also certain things that do reciprocate as to implication of existence in relation to others may be said to be prior to them, namely whenever they are the cause of their existence; and, in that case, it is reasonable to consider that the former are *naturally* prior to the latter. In this text,

DOI: 10.4324/9781003563266-3

therefore, it is through the fifth sense that the notion of priority by nature intervenes;[3] and, consequently, it is also this way that a certain notion of simultaneity, the one relevant to the relatives, turns out to be characterised as φύσει too.[4] In the presentation of *Cat.* 13, natural simultaneity construed this way is followed by another type of simultaneity, also called "natural", which constitutes the third sense of simultaneity distinguished in the chapter, namely that which applies to the coordinated species of the same genus (14b33–15a7).[5] However, at the end of the chapter, Aristotle makes it clear that the two types of natural simultaneity, though different, are opposed *en bloc* to the stricter sense of simultaneity, temporal simultaneity (15a7–12). This is indicative that, for him, temporal simultaneity and natural simultaneity (no matter now its own subtypes) correspond to distinct ways of being simultaneous, neither of which can be reduced to the other.

In terms of the relevant sense of natural simultaneity described in *Cat.* 13, two items *x* and *y* are, therefore, naturally simultaneous, when: (1) *x* and *y* reciprocate as to implication of existence; and (2) neither *x* is the cause of the existence of *y*, nor *y* is the cause of the existence of *x*. Hence, there is a failure of natural simultaneity, in this sense, if *x* and *y* reciprocate as to implication of existence, but *the cause of the existence* of *x* is *y*, or vice versa. In other words, *x* and *y* will not be naturally simultaneous if, despite the fact that, if *x* exists, *y* also exists, and vice versa, *y* exists *because* of *x*, or vice versa. Now, this gives us also an important hint about how Aristotle thinks of natural simultaneity, in this sense, as *natural* simultaneity. This hint could be represented thus: two things are naturally *simultaneous* if their respective existences imply each other; and they will be *naturally* simultaneous if the existence of neither causally depends on the existence of the other. This is, as we have seen, particularly suggested by the reasoning that, throughout chapter 12, leads Aristotle to the fifth sense of priority. That is to say, although reciprocation as to implication of existence constitutes, in itself, a factor for two things to be regarded as simultaneous in some nontemporal way,[6] it seems as if, here, Aristotle considers particularly fit to call this type of simultaneity "*natural* simultaneity" whenever this factor is joined with the second, causal condition. And the reason for this appears to be that for him it would make no sense to call two things "naturally simultaneous" when one of them must be presupposed to be *naturally prior to* the other, being the cause of its existence.[7]

3.2 Natural Simultaneity: The Causal Condition

In chapter 13, Aristotle does not explain the second condition he requires for natural simultaneity. He does not explain it either when he introduces this same condition as an additional reason for something to be called prior to something else in chapter 12. He gives there instead an example of things that, although reciprocating as to implication of existence, are causally linked, namely a certain fact and the true statement about it: the fact and the true statement do reciprocate as to implication of existence, but it is the fact that makes the statement true and not the other way around; and for this reason the former must be said to be naturally prior to the latter.[8]

Yet, if one considers specifically the relatives, it doesn't seem hard to think of other examples he could have been contemplating. Cases like the pair of relatives parent/child, in which the two relatives reciprocate as to implication of existence (if there is, for instance, a relative-father, there is a relative-child, and if there is a relative-child, there is a relative-father), but in which, however, one of them is the cause of the existence of the other, come easily to mind.[9] In fact, in this case, the two relatives, although reciprocating as to implication of existence, are clearly not simultaneous by nature, because the father, being the cause of the child's existence, is, for that reason, prior *by nature* to him. Therefore, if the second condition was ignored, cases such as these would (wrongly) be recognised as instances of natural simultaneity. It could be precisely this type of mistaken labelling that Aristotle wanted to avoid.

One might object that references to the father/child pair in the context of Aristotelian discussions of relatives are scant, at best: there is only one, to be exact, given in *Metaphysics* V 15.[10] Compare with the pairs double/half or knowledge/ knowable, by far the ones with the highest number of occurrences in this same context: in a non-exhaustive count, about 27 occurrences for the first and 21 for the second; or even with the master/slave pair, with no less than 5 occurrences.[11] However, this would of course be a self-refuting objection, since it does not exclude, but, on the contrary, acknowledges, that Aristotle thinks of this pair as a pair *of relatives*; and, given the peculiar nature of the complete notion of natural simultaneity in *Cat.* 13, one might even reasonably think, as suggested earlier, that Aristotle was led to it by reflecting on this kind of relatives.

Porphyry and subsequent Neoplatonic commentators would, no doubt, disagree with this interpretation. In particular, the extant Neoplatonic commentaries on the *Categories* that extend to the post-predicaments show that their authors are perfectly aware of the double condition that Aristotle requires there for natural simultaneity; however, strangely enough, when they come to apply this notion to relatives, following Aristotle's discussion of this issue in *Cat.* 7, they all (with the notable exception of Olympiodorus) give the father/child pair as an example of relatives that *are* simultaneous by nature.[12]

Porphyry, whose preserved catechetical commentary goes only as far as chapter 9, is already an evident testimony to this:

> For instance, a father is a father when taken together with his child, for it is together with his child that he possesses the being of a father, and a person comes to be a father when he comes to have a child. So "father" introduces "child" along with itself, and "child" introduces "father" along with itself. Conversely, without a child there cannot be a father, nor can there be a father without a child. Therefore, since "father" and "child" introduce each other, and when one is eliminated the other is as well, these will be simultaneous by nature.[13]

This exegetical decision is, however, especially challenging in the case of Ammonius, who, in his commentary on *Cat.* 7, twice recognises that there is a causal relationship between father and child,[14] while his comments on the relevant parts of *Cat.* 12 and 13 show that he is perfectly aware that causal relationship implies, for Aristotle, the natural non-simultaneity of the two relatives and, in fact, the natural priority of the relative-cause over the correlative-caused.[15] And the same thing occurs with Philoponus[16] and Simplicius.[17]

One might try to justify the commentators' position at this point by saying that it is the substance-father that is the cause of the substance-child's existence and not the relative-father that is the cause of the relative-child's existence.[18] Could this be the right way to look at the matter?

Clearly, the crucial point to respond to this question depends on what Aristotle means by "cause of existence" (αἴτιον τοῦ εἶναι). Unfortunately, he does not give us any explicit explanation of this concept. He provides us however with an important clue, namely the example he gives for the fifth sense of priority by nature, the reciprocation between a fact and the true statement about it. Although, he reasons, if a certain fact obtains in the world the statement that asserts it is true as well as if a certain statement is true the fact it asserts obtains, still the statement is true *because* the fact obtains, not the reverse.

So, the first thing to be noticed here is that when Aristotle speaks of "cause of existence" in this context he is not contemplating the activity of any causal power being exercised by one of the two reciprocating items over the other. The fact does not make the statement that asserts it true by doing anything, let alone by influencing or intervening in any way in it; in a strict sense, it does not even cause it to be true. Aristotle expressively uses the phrase "being *in some way* the cause of the other's existence" (τὸ αἴτιον ὁπωσοῦν θατέρῳ τοῦ εἶναι) to emphasise that, in cases such as these, although the existence of each item implies that of the other, the existence of one of them *is grounded* in the existence of the other.

Now, the appeal of the interpretation that could justify the commentators' position we are currently assessing is that it is quite evidently the substance-father (for example, Sophroniscus) who is the efficient cause of the substance-child (for example, Socrates) and, in this sense, the cause of his existence. But when we look at the example given in *Cat.* 12 we realise that it is not this type of causation Aristotle has in mind when he characterises there the second condition of natural priority. What he has in mind is more akin to metaphysical grounding than to efficient causality, in Aristotelian terms.[19]

So, if we now apply the pattern given by Aristotle's example to our issue, we are led to the conclusion that, as far as the father/child relationship is concerned, the point he would like to make is that, although the relative-father and the relative-child reciprocate as to implication of existence, the latter only exists *because* of the former – with the efficient causal relationship between the substances that are father and child to each other having nothing to do with the matter. Sophroniscus is indeed the cause of Socrates and therefore Socrates exists because of Sophroniscus; but the reason why the pair of relatives father/child is not naturally simultaneous lies not in this biological fact, but in the metaphysical notion that the existence of the child is grounded in the existence of the father.[20]

Hence, in the relevant sense, it is *as a father*, and therefore *as a relative*, that a father is the cause of his child's existence. Sophroniscus is of course the cause of Socrates' existence; however, in the relevant sense, it is not as Sophroniscus that he is the cause of Socrates' existence, but as his father. The question here bears on the grounding link between the existence of the two relatives, not on the causal link between the two substances in which they inhere. Additionally, it should be noted that it is precisely by being the (efficient) cause of Socrates' existence (only then and for that reason), that Sophroniscus becomes (his) father, that is, that he acquires this relational property, and that, thus, the relative-father (and, simultaneously, the correlative-child) comes about. The moment of efficient causation is, in other words, the moment that initiates correlativity (and therefore reciprocity); and this, from a different point of view, also bears witness to the fact that, in relatives such as these, it is as relatives that one is cause and the other is caused in the sense relevant to appraise their priority/posteriority or simultaneity relations.

Now, it could have conceivably been to avoid a hasty and mistaken application of the notion of natural simultaneity in cases like these that Aristotle introduced the restrictive clause: it is not enough to reciprocate as to implication of existence for two things to be considered simultaneous by nature; in addition to that, neither can be the cause of the other's existence. Thus, parent and child, for instance, certainly reciprocate as to implication of existence. But, according to the established notion of natural simultaneity, this is only a necessary, not a sufficient, condition for declaring them to be simultaneous by nature. The other necessary condition – that neither of them is the cause of the other's existence – does not obtain in this case. And, since only the two conditions are jointly sufficient, it follows, in this case, that parent and child are not simultaneous by nature.

3.3 Natural Simultaneity: Reciprocation as to Implication of Existence

Having considered the second condition of natural simultaneity, in the relevant sense, let us now focus on the first condition, reciprocation as to implication of existence, and let us think about it specifically in its application to relatives, which is the aspect that we need to explore. How is this condition to be interpreted in this case?

Two distinctions are surely key. We have, first of all, to distinguish between (a) correlativity, (b) reciprocity, and (c) reciprocation as to implication of existence; for, according to Aristotle, all relatives satisfy the first and second, but only some satisfy the third. Secondly, in view of what we saw above, the items that have to reciprocate as to implication of existence for the first condition of natural simultaneity to be met are *the relatives themselves*, not the subjects of which they are properties; what must reciprocate as to implication of existence is, for example, double and half, not the things that are double and half of each other, or master and slave, not the primary substances that reciprocally maintain the corresponding relations with each other.

Furthermore, it is worth explaining how reciprocation as to implication of existence ought to be conceived and formulated. Using the examples: reciprocation as to implication of existence does not simply obtain between double and half, but between *this* double and *its* half and between *this* half and *its* double (or, in other words: between the double of this half and the half of this double); and not simply between master and slave, but between this master and his slave and between this slave and his master (or, in other words: between the master of this slave and the slave of this master).[21] The second example illustrates very well the risks of not complying with this specification: otherwise, a master would not reciprocate as to implication of existence with each and every one of his slaves, because he would begin to be a master with the acquisition of the first slave and only cease to be one with the loss of the last one. This specification is, of course, a direct consequence of the notion of relative: each relative has *its* correlative, because it is *in relation* to this correlative that it is said to be just what it is. Moreover, this is utterly consistent with the fact that relatives are properties of *a certain* subject – properties that are always relative to the correlative ones in *a certain* other subject. Therefore, there is not really a master who has several slaves; as a relative, the master is the master of *that* slave (and the slave, conversely, is the slave of *that* master). The one who has several slaves is the *substance*-master, which only means that the same substance has several relations of the same type with several substances (several substances-*slave*); and it is only in view of this fact that, for simplicity's sake, it is said (but should be avoided) that the master has several slaves.

If one gives it some thought, this is much more straightforward than it appears at first. Each father is fatherly related to someone specifically; not to humanity in general, nor to no one particularly. Socrates is the father of Lamprocles, Menexenus and Sophroniscus; he is not a father, period. This technically means that Socrates has the property of being the-father-of-Lamprocles and the property of being the-father-of-Menexenus. Those are different properties, since in virtue of each of them Socrates is related to different subjects. In fact, as we saw earlier, a relational property is that by which the subject that bears it is related to another subject, namely the one that bears the correlative property.[22] So, each subject can, and regularly does, have many different relational properties of the same type, many different properties of being the-father-of-X, for example: as many as the children that the person in question has; in general, as many as the relations that the subject has.

Bearing these warnings in mind, let us now try to spell out how reciprocation as to implication of existence should be interpreted in Aristotelian terms, specifically in the case of relatives. This is a task that is very rarely seen in the literature (Duncombe 2020, to which I will turn right away, is a commendable exception),[23] a direct consequence of the relative lack of interest that the issue of natural simultaneity of relatives has generally received on the part of commentators, both ancient and (especially) modern, on chapter 7 of the *Categories*.

To do so, let us start by recalling the rules of correlativity and reciprocity of relatives previously formulated:

> *RC = Every relative has a correlative, in relation to which it is said to be what it is.*
>
> *RR = If a relative is said to be R of its correlative, the latter is said to be R' of the former (R' being the reciprocal relation of R).*

Considering these two rules, it is obvious that the rule of reciprocation as to implication of existence of relatives (RRIE) must be, for Aristotle, not only different from these rules, but also *narrower and more robust* than them, insofar as, according to him, there are relatives that satisfy RC and RR, but do not satisfy RRIE. This fact allows us to immediately discard the interpretation recently proposed by Duncombe, which he himself justifiably qualifies as "weak".[24] Indeed, according to that interpretation, RRIE is a simple consequence of RC and applies to everything to which it applies; hence, according to this interpretation, *all* relatives satisfy RRIE (and therefore, as Duncombe hastily concludes, they are all naturally simultaneous). In his own terms:

> I suggest that a relative and correlative are naturally simultaneous in the sense that if you admit one into your ontology, then you must admit the other too. If you admit that there is a double, then

> you must admit that there is a half too; if you admit that there is a master, then you must admit that there is a slave too.[25]

Clearly, in terms of this interpretation, reciprocation as to implication of existence is practically reduced to correlativity.[26] However, Aristotle has just discussed reciprocity, which presupposes and reinforces correlativity, when he introduces the issue of the natural simultaneity of relatives. Now, if this interpretation were right, then Aristotle would be, at this point, unexpectedly and without notice turning back to the initial description of relatives, which is odd, and treating it as if it were simply another feature of them, among others, which is odder. On the other hand, and more importantly, Duncombe's interpretation, as we have seen, has the consequence that natural simultaneity, thus understood (and in fact reduced to reciprocation as to implication of existence), applies to all relatives. However, Aristotle makes it abundantly clear in *Cat.* 7 that he considers there to be several powerful arguments against the application of RRIE to all relatives. Therefore, Duncombe's interpretation is not the one we need to understand the Aristotelian position here.

Duncombe makes an important interpretative point though. As we saw earlier, Aristotle carefully distinguishes between natural and temporal simultaneity. However, the most common interpretation of the former (for example, that of the ancient commentators) implicitly conceives it as coexistence at all the same times. Now, to interpret natural simultaneity in this way means to construe it as a mere modality of temporal simultaneity. Therefore, this interpretation cannot be right.[27] Furthermore, we have already seen that certain puzzles of correlativity and reciprocity of relatives seem to imply the existence of temporally *asymmetrical* relations, which also collides with the interpretation of natural simultaneity as coexistence at all the same times. Indeed, in these cases, the relatives (for example, the aforementioned cases of master/slave or father/child) are simultaneous by nature, but not in time.

How then to conceive, in proper Aristotelian terms, reciprocation as to implication of existence in the case of relatives – and, so, in such a way that the corresponding rule can be seen as going beyond RC and RR? I propose that it be read as follows: for two relatives x and y to reciprocate as to implication of existence it is necessary and sufficient that, if x begins to exist as x, y also begins to exist as y, and vice versa, and if x ceases to exist as x, so does y cease to exist as y, and vice versa.[28] An example: a certain double and a certain half relative to each other reciprocate as to implication of existence if and only if, if the double begins to exist as a double, its half begins to exist as a half, and vice versa, and if the double ceases to exist as a double, its half ceases to exist as a half, and vice versa. The same holds if the relatives are now master and slave: both reciprocate as to implication of existence, because, if the master begins to exist as a master, his slave begins to exist as slave, and vice versa, and if the master ceases to exist as a master, his slave ceases to exist as a slave, and vice versa.

We can therefore formulate now our new rule as follows:

> *RRIE = If a relative begins to exist as R of its correlative, the latter begins to exist as R' of the former, and vice versa; and if a relative ceases to exist as R of its correlative, the latter ceases to exist as R' of the former, and vice versa.*[29]

The decisive question to verify whether, under this formula, RRIE may be interpreted as making a narrower and more robust requirement than those made by RC and RR, as Aristotle's position on the problematic pairs requires, seems, then, to be the following: considering this interpretation, in which cases do RC and RR obtain, but not RRIE? The fact, however, is that we don't need to ask this. What we do need to ask is rather: given this interpretation, what cases would *Aristotle* conceive of as satisfying RC and RR but not RRIE? Now, whatever one may think about the validity of the Aristotelian position in this respect, such cases are explicitly identified in the text of *Cat.* 7: the pairs knowledge/knowable and perception/perceptible. Does the proposed interpretation allow to give this position a plausible and reasonable (though not necessarily unobjectionable) tenor? The answer is unequivocally "yes". As we will have the opportunity to see directly and at length in the next chapter, an essential part of Aristotle's position regarding the failure of natural simultaneity of those problematic pairs can be stated thus (fully observing the terms of the proposed interpretation): the knowable begins to exist as *R* of its correlative (knowledge) *before* knowledge begins to exist as *R'* of the relative (the knowable). More clearly: the knowable begins to exist as knowable by some knowledge before such knowledge begins to exist as knowledge of that knowable.[30] And the same can be said, mutatis mutandis, of the pair perception/perceptible. Now, if both knowledge and the knowable, like perception and the perceptible, are relatives, as

Aristotle repeatedly says they are,[31] then they are necessarily subject to RC and RR. The proposed interpretation of RRIE, therefore, gives prima facie room for a conception, as the Aristotelian one, in which RC and RR obtain, but RRIE does not; and it does this by allowing, as required, RRIE to be read as a narrower and more robust rule than RC and RR.[32]

This said, we can now propose a deflationary interpretation of what "exist" means in the expressions "begin to exist" and "cease to exist" contained in RRIE, through the following reformulation of this rule:

> *RRIE² = If a relative comes to be R of its correlative, the latter comes to be R' of the former, and vice versa; and if a relative ceases to be R of its correlative, the latter ceases to be R' of the former, and vice versa.*

In addition to the linguistic advantage of this formulation being closer to the original text, in which the verb "to exist" is obviously missing, it has the philosophical advantage of eliminating any kind of strong existential implication of the key notions, namely come to be *R* (respectively, *R'*) and cease to be *R* (respectively, *R'*). On this new formulation, "begin to be" and "cease to be" simply mean, respectively, to start to be and to stop being *a relative*, and therefore to start to be and stop being *relatively* to something else. Applying this reformulation to examples of cases in which RRIE obtains and to examples of cases in which, according to Aristotle, it does not: if a certain double begins to be (or, respectively, ceases to be) a double, its half begins to be (or, respectively, ceases to be) a half, and vice versa; but a certain knowable may begin to be knowable by some knowledge before some knowledge begins to be knowledge of that knowable.

One might say: but doesn't this, after all, revert to the solution proposed by Duncombe 2020? No, because, on the present interpretation, the limits of natural simultaneity are determined by the beginning and ceasing to be *of the relatives themselves*, not by their recognition as relatives (or, in Duncombe's terms, by their "admission into our ontology"). And this difference is all that it takes to allow, at least theoretically, failures of RRIE in cases that satisfy RC and RR, which Duncombe's solution does not allow.

Another question that could be raised is whether RRIE, interpreted in this way, does not have the consequence of reducing natural simultaneity, of which this rule expresses the first condition, to a subtype of temporal simultaneity. The answer is, again, "no", for two reasons. First, what the rule stipulates are the conditions under which two relatives come into existence and cease to exist, not their coexistence at all the same times. Second, even if RRIE, and therefore natural simultaneity, implied coexistence at all the same times (which, if the notion of temporally asymmetrical relation introduced earlier is sound and instantiated, does not seem to be the case), it would not be *because* two relatives coexist at all the same times that they would be *naturally* simultaneous, but because they reciprocate as to implication of existence in the sense indicated.

Notes

1 Compare, for example, the enunciation of the senses of "per se" in *APo.* I 4, or the enunciation of the senses of "being" in *Metaph.* V 7.

2 Cf. 12, 14b10–13: "There would seem, however, to be another manner of priority besides those mentioned. For of things which reciprocate as to implication of existence, that which is in some way the cause of the other's existence (τὸ αἴτιον ὁπωσοῦν θατέρῳ τοῦ εἶναι) might reasonably be called prior by nature."

3 Although the fourth sense of priority, referred to by Aristotle as "perhaps the least proper" (ἀλλοτριώτατος) (14b7), had already been described as being "by nature" (14b4–5). This fourth sense concerns "what is better and more valued" (τὸ βέλτιον καὶ τὸ τιμιώτερον); the rationale of calling this type of priority "natural priority" must be that things deemed as more valuable than others are perceived as having an intrinsic precedence over them.

4 Priority in the second sense listed in *Cat.* 12 (not reciprocating as to implication of existence) is referred to again in a few places outside the *Categories*, sometimes under the designation of "priority in respect of nature and substance" (*Metaph.* V 11, 1019a1–4, its use being attributed to Plato), sometimes under the designation of "priority in substance" (*Metaph.* XIII 2, 1077b2–3), sometimes without any specific designation (*Ph.* VIII 7, 260b17–19). Priority by nature is mentioned again, without any details, in *Ph.* VIII 9, 265a22 (and see further "priority in being" in *Metaph.* VII 15, 1040a21–22). I leave undecided the question of whether the priority χρόνῳ of substance referred to in *Metaph.* VII I, 1028a31–34, should also be listed under this second sense of priority, or at least whether the claim made by Aristotle in lines 33–34 that only substance is separate should be interpreted in this way, as Peramatzis 2011: 230–253 has recently argued.

5 The same notion occurs at *Top.* VI 9, 147b7–10.

6 And remember that Aristotle even calls elsewhere (though not, significantly, in the *Categories*) non-reciprocation as to implication of existence "priority in respect *of nature* and substance" (see above, note 4).

7 In their analysis of chapter 7, the majority of commentators, both ancient and modern, have tended to neglect the second condition and to consider only the first, as if natural simultaneity, in the relevant sense, were simply the same as reciprocation as to implication of existence. But this is formally precluded by the text of *Cat.* 13 that we have just recalled and where the relevant notion is officially fixed. As we have seen (above, Chapter 1, note 24), among modern commentators, Caston 2018: 39–40n8 and Edelhoff 2020: 34, 39–41 are relevant exceptions here.

8 Cf. *Cat.* 12, 14b9–24.

9 Aristotle does not give this as an example of relatives in the *Categories*, but he does so in the *Metaphysics* V 15, 1021a23–25.

10 The same, by the way, happens with Plato: this pair occurs only once as an example of relatives, namely in the *Symposium* 199de (but see also *Euthd.* 297e-299a).

11 It is worth noticing that this scarcity contrasts sharply with the ancient and modern commentary of the chapter, where this example is strongly prevalent. For example, in the section of Porphyry's commentary, the pair occurs seven times; in Ammonius', five; in Philoponus', twelve; in Simplicius', seventeen; in the extant extract from the anonymous Syriac catechetical commentary, three; in Sergius of Reshaina's introduction, four, in less than three pages (this is the most recurrent example of relatives given in this very short text), while in his commentary the pair appears six times. On the contrary, Averroes, in his middle commentary on *Cat.* 7, never uses this example. But in Thomas Aquinas there are several occurrences of the pair, for example: *Summa Theologica* I q. 13 a. 7; I q. 28 a. 4; *Scriptum super libros Sententiarum* I d. 27 q. 1 a. 1 ad 2; the same goes with Duns Scotus: see *Quaestiones super Praedicamenta Aristotelis* q. 27, 4–7, and q. 29, 20–21. As far as the extant texts allow us to ascertain, it seems to have been Plotinus who first gave this pair the centrality that it would later acquire in Aristotle's ancient commentary, by mentioning it at the beginning of his treatment of relatives, along with some of the most classic Aristotelian examples of relatives (namely double/half, as well as master/slave, but also state, condition, position, equal, similar, measure/measurable and even knowledge/knowable, perception/perceptible, etc.): see VI.1.6.6–17. However, the frequency of the example may occur already in the Stoics, if the examples that Simplicius mentions in his description of the Stoic theory of relativity (*In Cat.* 165.33–166.29 Kalbfleisch) are also theirs.

12 See Ammonius, *In Cat.* 76.10–17 Busse; Philoponus, *In Cat.* 122.27–30 Busse (who follows Ammonius here almost to the letter; but cf.

already 114.23–24 and again 130.12–19); Simplicius, *In Cat.* 190.1–30 Kalbfleisch; Elias, *In Cat.* 213.26–31 Busse; Boethius, *In Cat.* 228bc and 230ab Migne; Sergius of Reshaina, *Introd.* §§ 75, 78 and 79 Aydin. The same also applies to Thomas Aquinas: cf. *Summa Theologica* I q. 13 a. 7 ad 6. According to DelCogliano 2010: 227–234, Christian theology of the third century, from Origen onwards, took exactly this same path in its doctrine of the first two persons of the Trinity, concluding from it the coeternity of the Father and the Son.

13 *In Cat.* 118.8–13 Busse; Strange's translation.

14 Cf. 67.23 and 76.14–15 (the latter excerpt occurs in the very passage in which Ammonius gives this pair of relatives as an example of natural simultaneity).

15 And note that, in his commentary on *Cat.* 12, Ammonius even uses the father/son pair as an example of priority by nature in the fifth sense. See, on *Cat.* 12, 104.2–5: "For if, Aristotle says, one of the reciprocals were the cause of the existence of the other, it would rightly be called prior. For example, a father is the father of a son, but they reciprocate with each other: the son is the son of the father. If, then, the father is the cause of the existence of the son, he would rightly be called prior in nature to the son." And, on *Cat.* 13, see 104.19–105.1: "Since Aristotle mentioned the simultaneous in his teaching on the categories, he also discusses it here. Just as we said about priority, that its first meaning, strictly speaking, is with respect to time, so also here, Aristotle says. Nature is second, just as was also said about the former. This sense is opposed to the second and fifth senses of priority, for with them there is a converse implication of existence and neither is the cause of the other's existence." (Both translations by Cohen/Matthews.)

16 He too recognises that there is a causal relationship between father and son (105.9) and his comments on the relevant parts of *Cat.* 12 and 13 (194.8–25 and 195.27–196.17, respectively) show that he is aware of the second condition of natural simultaneity (being that, in both comments, he uses the father/son pair as an example). The only difference with Ammonius is that Philoponus does not incorporate any reference to the causal character of the relationship between father and son in his use of this pair as an example of natural simultaneity of relatives.

17 See his comments on the relevant parts of *Cat.* 12 and 13, respectively, at 421.1–10 (also giving the father/son pair as an example) and 424.14–23.

18 This argument is hinted at, though not fully expressed, by Sergius of Reshaina, *Introd.* § 78 Aydin (and cf. *In Cat.* 340 Arzhanov). It is possible that it also underlies the commentaries of Ammonius (*In Cat.* 76.10–17 Busse) and Philoponus (*In Cat.* 122.23–30 Busse).

19 For metaphysical grounding in Aristotle, in a different though related context, see Corkum 2016.

20 Note further that αἴτιον, which Ackrill translates here as "cause" (a translation I have, after consideration, retained) is generally, in Aristotle, a somewhat less technical term than αἰτία. This agrees well with the adverb ὁπωσοῦν, "in any way whatsoever". Perhaps a better, more neutral translation of Aristotle's phrase αἴτιον ὁπωσοῦν θατέρῳ τοῦ εἶναι would be: "responsible in whatever way for the being of the other" ("in whatever way" meaning including, but not necessarily according to one of the four causes).

21 The analysis by Mendelsohn 2019: 39–40 also seems to be oriented in this direction. And recall, for a context, Chapter 2, note 16.

22 See, *supra*, chapter 2.1.

23 As mentioned in note 2 in chapter 1, Edelhoff 2020: 34–50 is, of course, another exception. For an older treatment of the issue, see Cleary 1988: 25–32 and, from a particular perspective, Gottlieb 1993.

24 Duncombe 2020: 117 (text quoted below, note 26).

25 Duncombe 2020: 108. The quoted text clearly shows that Duncombe disregards the second condition of natural simultaneity; so, when he speaks of natural simultaneity, he is in fact speaking of reciprocation as to implication of existence.

26 This becomes almost explicit in the following passage: "I interpreted Aristotle's natural simultaneity, an ontological dependence relation that obtains between correlatives, weakly – *it amounts to the claim that if there is a relative, then there must be its correlative*." (Duncombe 2020: 117; italics mine.)

27 See Duncombe 2020: 107–108. From an opposite perspective, Edelhoff 2020, although not reducing natural to temporal simultaneity, argues that the former includes the latter (cf. 35–36, 39, 49), an interpretation that not only does not seem in any way necessitated by the text, but is also contradicted by the reasons given in the paragraph.

28 To say that a certain relative begins or ceases to exist *as a relative* is, of course, ultimately redundant. The additional specification is not superfluous though, for it becomes useful when analysing how the rule applies to concrete examples, in particular the problematic pairs. I use it therefore as an emphatic formula. Some such formulae will keep coming up until the end of this chapter and sporadically in the next, for the same reason.

29 A question could be raised about how, on this account, RRIE is ever satisfied in eternal or atemporal relations. The answer is that it can be satisfied by stipulating that, by definition, eternal or atemporal relatives have, in any moment in time, always begun to exist and will, in no moment in time, cease to exist. The corollary of this stipulation is that all such relatives reciprocate as to implication of existence with their correlatives. This stipulation (but not necessarily, at least in Aristotle's eyes, the corollary) remains valid if the relation is between relatives only one of which

is eternal or atemporal, as is typically the case with knowledge of eternal truths.

30 It could be argued that, strictly speaking, one should always speak, contrary to how I did in the text, of knowledge as relative and knowable as correlative, if this pair is indeed to be seen as *intentional*. On the most frequent interpretation of the text, this is what Aristotle maintains in *Metaph.* V 15, 1021a26–b3 (but see my own comment on this text in Chapter 5.3, below). Using Porphyry's vocabulary, one could therefore say that in cases like these it is always fixed beforehand what is the "first term" (*In Cat.* 115.19–28 Busse; or the ἀφ' οὗ, the "from which": 112.9) and what is the "second term" (or the πρὸς ὅν: 112.10) of the relation. However, it is evident that, in the strict terms of RR, it is indifferent which is the relative and which is the correlative in these cases too.

31 See again note 25 in Chapter 1.

32 Whether this reading is a legitimate one or not is a different question, which I will address later, in Chapter 4.3.

4 Natural Simultaneity of Relatives

4.1 The Text of *Cat.* 7, 7b15–8a12

We are finally in a position to directly confront the pertinent text of *Cat.* 7. It reads thus:

> *[I]* Relatives seem to be simultaneous by nature and in most cases this is true. *[II]* For double and half are simultaneous, *[II A]* and if there is a half there is a double, and if there is a slave there is a master; and similarly with the others. *[II B]* Also, one carries the other to destruction; for if there is not a double there is not a half, and if there is not a half there is not a double. So too with other such cases. *[III]* Yet it does not seem to be true of all relatives that they are simultaneous by nature. *[IV]* For the knowable would seem to be prior to knowledge. *[IV A]* For as a rule it is of actual things already existing that we acquire knowledge; in few cases, if any, could one find knowledge coming into existence at the same time as what is knowable. *[IV B]* Moreover, destruction of the knowable carries knowledge to destruction, but [the destruction of] knowledge does not carry the knowable to destruction. For if there is not a knowable there is not knowledge – there will no longer be anything for knowledge to be of – but if there is not knowledge there is nothing to prevent there being a knowable. Take, for example, the squaring of the circle, supposing it to be knowable; knowledge of it does not yet exist but the knowable itself exists. *[IV C]* Again, if animal is destroyed there is no knowledge, but there may be many knowables. *[V]* The case of perception is similar to this; the perceptible seems to be prior to perception. *[V A]* For the destruction of the perceptible carries perception to destruction, but [that of]

DOI: 10.4324/9781003563266-4

> perception does not carry the perceptible to destruction. *[V A 1]* For perceptions are to do with body and in body, and if the perceptible is destroyed, body too is destroyed (since body is itself a perceptible), and if there is not body, perception too is destroyed; hence [the destruction of] the perceptible carries perception to destruction. *[V A 2]* But [the destruction of] perception does not carry the perceptible [to destruction]. For if animal is destroyed perception is destroyed, but there will be something perceptible, such as body, hot, sweet, bitter, and all the other perceptibles. *[V B]* Moreover, perception comes into existence at the same time as what is capable of perceiving – an animal and perception come into existence at the same time – but the perceptible exists even before perception exists; fire and water and so on, of which an animal is itself made up, exist even before there exists an animal at all, or perception. Hence the perceptible would seem to be prior to perception.

The structure of the excerpt is relatively straightforward. After stating the general thesis, that relatives seem to be simultaneous by nature and that in most cases this is true *[I]*, and giving some examples where this is in fact true *[II]*, Aristotle notes that it does not seem that this is always the case *[III],* devoting his attention to two apparent exceptions: first, the knowledge/knowable pair *[IV]*; and then the perception/perceptible pair *[V]*. In both cases, the reason why the two members of each pair do not appear to be simultaneous by nature is the same: because the second member of each pair appears to be *prior* to the first.[1]

In the section on knowledge and the knowable, Aristotle advances three arguments to support the priority of the latter over the former. The first argument *[IV A]* is presented very succinctly, so it requires some reconstruction work. I suppose the idea is as follows: (i) as a general rule, what comes to be known at a certain moment already exists before it is known; (ii) however, if it comes to be known, then, before being known, it was already knowable (implicit premise); (iii) ergo, the knowable is, as a general rule, prior to knowledge.[2] The second argument *[IV B]* is much more clearly presented, and it implicitly mobilises the notion of reciprocation as to implication of existence. We can state it as follows: (i) things that, by ceasing to exist, imply that others cease to exist, while the converse is not the case, are prior by nature to these (implicit premise); (ii) now, if the knowable ceases to exist, knowledge ceases to exist ("destruction of the knowable carries knowledge to destruction": 7b27–28), since, without something knowable, "there will no longer be anything for knowledge to be of" (7b29–30); (iii) nonetheless, the converse is not true, since, if knowledge is destroyed, the knowable is not necessarily destroyed ("[destruction of] knowledge does not carry the knowable to destruction": 7b28–29), insofar as, "if there is not knowledge, there is nothing to prevent there being a knowable" (7b30–31);[3] (iv) ergo, the knowable is by nature prior to knowledge. The third argument *[IV C]* is more of a complement to the previous one and works on the same reasoning as it, on which it partially rests: (i) given that only animals know (implicit), "if animal is destroyed, there is no knowledge" (7b33–34); (ii) nonetheless, animal being destroyed, "there may be many knowables" (7b34–35); (iii) hence, the elimination of animal, and, with it, of knowledge, does not entail the elimination of the knowable; (iv) but, by the preceding argument, the elimination of the knowable entails the elimination of knowledge (implicit premise); (v) ergo, the knowable is by nature prior to knowledge.[4]

Then come two arguments to support the priority of the perceptible over perception. The first argument *[V A]* is the counterpart of *IV B*: "the destruction of the perceptible carries perception to destruction, but [that of] perception does not carry the perceptible to destruction" (7b36–38). However, the argument offered here is more complex and comprises two sub-arguments. The first one *[V A 1]* intends to prove that the elimination of the perceptible entails the elimination of perception; the second *[V A 2]*, that the elimination of perception does not entail the elimination of the perceptible. The first sub-argument, which is more difficult and controversial, seems to be the following: (i) all bodies are perceptible (8a1); (ii) on the other hand, perceptions exist in bodies (7b39); (iii) then, if all perceptibles are eliminated, all bodies are also eliminated (7b39–8a1), including those where perceptions exist; (iv) therefore, if all perceptibles are eliminated, perceptions are also eliminated (8a1–2); (v) ergo, the elimination of the perceptible entails the elimination of perception (8a2–3). The second sub-argument is as follows: (i) since only animals perceive (implicit), if animal is eliminated, perception will be eliminated; (ii) however, if animal is eliminated, many perceptible things would continue to exist, without being thereby eliminated; (iii) ergo, the elimination of perception does not entail the elimination of the perceptible. The general conclusion of the argument is, as is required, that the perceptible is prior by nature to perception.[5] The second argument [V B] is shorter, but also more original. We can reconstruct it as follows: (i) the elements of which animal is composed, such as fire and water, are prior to it (8a9–11); (ii) but these elements are perceptible (8a8–9); (iii) on the contrary, perception only arises with the emergence of animals (8a7–8), because only animals are capable of perceiving (implicit); (iv) therefore, certain perceptibles, at least, are prior to perception (8a11–12).[6]

Two of the five arguments we have seen, *IV A* and *V B*, clearly adopt a different strategy than the rest. This difference has been attributed by several ancient commentators to the fact that such arguments are founded on the notion of temporal simultaneity and not on that of natural simultaneity.[7] In fact, a possibly suggestive aspect of Aristotle's discussion which goes in this direction (from a somewhat conspiratorial perspective) is that, in the enunciation of the two cases considered, Aristotle never makes clear in what sense, or senses, the knowable seems to be prior to knowledge and the perceptible prior to perception: "the knowable would seem to be *prior* to knowledge" (7b23–35); "the perceptible seems to be *prior* to perception" (7b36). However, this interpretation collides with the fundamental fact that Aristotle is *explicitly* considering here the *natural* simultaneity of relatives and not their temporal simultaneity. Furthermore, this interpretation seems to be suggested only by the way in which the arguments are formulated, and to rest, therefore, on a question of language,[8] without truly grasping their *modus operandi*. If, on the contrary, we keep in mind the reading of RRIE that I have earlier shown to be required by Aristotle's position on the problematic pairs,[9] this seems to be enough to understand the arguments, without making any appeal to temporal simultaneity. Indeed, the point of both arguments is that, as a rule, the knowable and the perceptible *begin to exist* as such before any knowledge and any perception begin to exist as knowledge and perception of them, so that they too function exclusively on the basis of the concept of reciprocation as to implication of existence, which is, as we have seen, an essential ingredient of natural simultaneity. This alternative interpretation is, moreover, strongly reinforced if we remember that all the other arguments seek to prove the failure of reciprocation as to implication of existence from the fact that knowledge and perception can *cease* to exist without, respectively, the knowable and the perceptible ceasing to exist, while the converse is not true. And, interpreted thus, Aristotle's line of reasoning is shown to have been deliberately designed to systematically cover the two aspects involved in RRIE and, hence, to present itself as complete and exhaustive: in the case of knowledge, first offering an argument based on the asynchrony of the beginning-to-exist of the two relatives, followed by two arguments based on the asynchrony of their ceasing-to-exist; in the case of perception, first offering an argument based on the asynchrony of the ceasing-to-exist of the two relatives, followed by another based on the asynchrony of their beginning-to-exist.[10]

4.2 Conceptual Clarifications

Before moving on to a careful analysis of these arguments, it is important to clarify some aspects of the key concepts involved in them: knowledge (ἐπιστήμη) and knowable (ἐπιστητόν), perception (αἴσθησις) and perceptible (αἰσθητόν). First of all, with reference to translation. As is well known, the terms ἐπιστητόν and αἰσθητόν, although originally meaning "knowable" and "perceptible", respectively, can also mean, in certain contexts, "known" and "perceived".[11] I take, however, for granted (as is usually done) that, in this context, they can only mean the first options. Indeed, if they meant respectively "known" and "perceived", Aristotle would not have had reason to question their natural simultaneity with, respectively, knowledge and perception: for knowledge and the known, like perception and the perceived, reciprocate without any doubt as to implication of existence, and therefore – if we assume that there is no causal nexus between the respective existences – they are simultaneous by nature in terms of the notion expounded in *Cat.* 13.[12] Aristotle is therefore using the terms ἐπιστητόν and αἰσθητόν at 7b15–8a12 in the senses of "knowable" and "perceptible", respectively. Incidentally, that is why it is common to find in modern commentators of this text the complain that Aristotle might have been able to preserve the universality of the application of the criterion of natural simultaneity to relatives if, instead of taking knowledge and the knowable as correlatives, on the one hand, and perception and the perceptible, on the other, he had respectively taken knowledge and the known and perception and the perceived.[13] This remark is pertinent – and it would even be unqualifiedly true if it were possible (as it is not) to abstract the restrictive clause of causality from the notion of natural simultaneity. That Aristotle apparently did not anticipate it and preferred to conceive in this text the correlatives of knowledge and perception as, respectively, the knowable and the perceptible is in itself a cause for perplexity, but one on which I will not dwell.[14]

There is, however, a philosophically more relevant question that should be addressed regarding the knowledge/knowable pair. What sort of thing does Aristotle have in mind when he speaks of "knowables"? More accurately put, what kind of things is he considering as possible subjects of inherence of such a relative? In fact, he does not seem to be thinking about objects, namely concrete objects, because, in his strategy of demonstrating the lack of simultaneity between knowledge and the knowable, he emphatically states, as we have seen, that when the knowable is destroyed, knowledge is also destroyed, while the converse is not true. Now, when a knowable *object* is destroyed, knowledge of it is not necessarily destroyed. For example, the physical disappearance of a person I have known does not entail the disappearance of my knowledge of her; far from it: I can represent her in my memory, continue to describe her in detail, etc. What he seems to have in mind are rather facts and/or states of affairs, in which the elimination of the thing to be known actually entails the elimination of knowledge; if something is shown not to be, after all, a fact or a state of affairs, there is no longer anything to know. Now, it is suggestive, in this regard, that the only example of a knowable thing that Aristotle gives throughout the text is the squaring of the circle, whose solution, if it were possible, would then be a scientific fact (or would rest on scientific facts). This gives us some indication about the notion of knowledge that is implicitly at work in the text. Firstly, as might have been guessed from his choice of words, Aristotle seems to be considering solely propositional knowledge and excluding any kind of acquaintance or procedural knowledge. Secondly, ἐπιστήμη does not seem to have here the meaning of knowledge in general, but a more restricted and probably more technical meaning, possibly corresponding to the meaning that the concept takes on in the *Posterior Analytics*.[15] Perhaps a generic and suitably cautious way of formulating the meaning underlying the word in this context is as follows: having ἐπιστήμη, in this sense, consists in apprehending a true proposition as such.

Clearly, no similar problem arises with regard to the pair perception/ perceptible. It should be noted, however, that, in this text, Aristotle seems to be using the term "perceptible" to refer to both the (concrete) object susceptible of being perceived and the sensible properties that it exemplifies – for instance, to use the text's own examples, to refer to both an object that is perceived as sweet and the perceptual property sweet itself. This, as we shall see, is not without relevance to grasping the train of thought behind this text.[16]

4.3 Analysing the Arguments

Bearing these aspects in mind, let us now evaluate the strength of the five arguments set forth by Aristotle and, consequently, that of the thesis they mean to support, namely the priority by nature of the knowable in relation to knowledge and of the perceptible in relation to perception, and, therefore, the exceptionality of these two pairs of relatives with regard to natural simultaneity, which, so it was assumed, most relatives share.

I intend to show that there are problems of various kinds in these arguments; and that, because of these problems, they fail to prove that thesis. To this end, a good entry point may be to fix how, in the light of the principles established by Aristotle regarding relatives, the thesis itself should be understood. Taking into account those principles, as previously construed, it seems evident that, as happens with all relatives, the relatives whose exceptionality is alleged are not knowledge in general and the knowables in general, nor perception in general and the perceptibles in general; they are, rather, knowledge *of that* knowable and, conversely, the knowable *by that* knowledge, as well as perception *of that* perceptible and, conversely, the perceptible *by that* perception. This precision follows directly from some very basic notions about the relatives, namely the very notion of correlativity: each relative is said to be just what it is in relation to its correlative – relative and correlative being properties of particular subjects, or "particular accidents", in the traditional nomenclature of the ontological square.[17] Yet, Aristotle sometimes speaks (blatantly, in *IV C*, *VA A*, and *V B*, arguments to which I will return in more detail in a moment) as if he were considering knowledge and the knowables *in general*, as well as perception and the perceptibles *in general*. This presents an obvious problem. Admittedly, not a very serious one, but, as we will see, some of its implications are.

On the other hand, the problem that I will discuss next is in itself a very serious one. According to the long analysis of the conditions of reciprocity that follows the statement of RR, reciprocity, and, with it, the relativity of relatives itself, is only assured if *the proper correlatives* are considered. Now, it seems clear that at least some of the arguments offered by Aristotle do not meet this requirement.

Which relatives should be considered the proper ones in these two cases? Clearly, the proper relatives are, on the one hand, a certain knowable and the knowledge by which that knowable is said to be knowable, and, on the other hand, a certain perceptible and the perception by which that perceptible is said to be perceptible. In general, then, the proper relatives are, in the one case, a certain knowable *x* and a certain knowledge of *x* (qua knowledge and knowable), in the other, a certain perceptible *y* and a certain perception of *y* (qua perception and perceptible). Now, this basic principle that governs the way to correctly construct relative pairs seems to be ignored in some of the arguments presented. This is especially clear in *IV B* and *V A*. In *IV B*, Aristotle states that, if the knowable is eliminated, knowledge will also be eliminated, but that the converse is not true, insofar as knowledge can be eliminated without the knowable being eliminated. However, these claims are ambiguous. And when the ambiguity is cleared up, the arguments fail. Indeed, to respect the basic principle indicated, what Aristotle would have to guarantee is that, if a certain knowable ceases to exist as such, the knowledge by which it is said to be knowable also ceases to exist, while some knowledge may cease to exist as knowledge of a knowable without that knowable ceasing to exist as knowable by that knowledge. Now, although the first claim is true, the second is not, because the knowable that may subsist in that circumstance will no longer be knowable *by that knowledge*. That is, in the situation described, the failure of reciprocation as to implication of existence, and, therefore, of natural simultaneity, which was pointed out, does not occur *between two correlatives*. But, if the failure does not occur between two correlatives, nothing follows from this observation for the issue of the natural simultaneity *of relatives*, nor for that of these two (knowledge/knowable) in particular. And, since we have seen that, despite the differences between the two, the kernel of *V A* is exactly the same as that of *IV B*, the same thing can be concluded about *V A*.[18]

In addition to this problem, argument *V A* also shares with *IV C* a kind of universalised – and, as such, aggravated – version of it. As we have seen, the common point between these two arguments is that, since animal is that by which there is knowledge and perception, if animals were eliminated, there would cease to be both knowledge and perception, without, however, there ceasing to be many knowables and many perceptibles. But this assertion is a bit disturbing. If knowledge and perception were eliminated, how *could* something come to be known or perceived (and this is what it means, respectively, to be knowable and to be perceptible: *to be able* to be known and *to be able* to be perceived), if being known or perceived consists precisely in being the object of knowledge and perception? More simply, how can something be described as knowable or perceptible unless faced with the prospect of possible knowledge and perception, and such a possibility is cancelled out by the very premises of the arguments? In fact, given what is assumed in these premises, on the hypothesis of the elimination of animals, all knowledge and all perception are also eliminated, since no being remains that is capable of knowing and perceiving. However, if the knowable is what can be known and the perceptible is what can be perceived, how can one accept, in this case, in which there no longer are beings able to know or perceive, that something continues to be described as knowable and perceptible? Again, more simply: how can anything be said to be knowable or perceptible unless there is something that can know or perceive it, and that is what the premises of the arguments declare no longer to be the case?[19]

One might object that this view of knowability and perceptibility is unduly restrictive – that, as a matter of fact, for something to be knowable it suffices that a mind capable of knowing *could* exist, even if there is currently none and there will never be one; and the same, mutatis mutandis, regarding something perceptible. I myself have argued along these lines in a discussion of a monograph on Aristotle's treatise on time.[20] This is indeed a valid point, but it has to be considered in conjunction with the special conditions that, by virtue of the doctrine of the ontological square, bind Aristotle when temporally asymmetrical relations involving the future are at stake. For, as we have seen, such relations require that, for something of which there is currently no correlative knowledge to be knowable *now*, there must be *actually* in the future some potential bearer of such knowledge.[21] Now, if we combine these two aspects, we are forced to conclude that, in order for Aristotle's position to be consistently upheld, it would be necessary for him to accept that, if animals were eliminated, future knowers would also be eliminated, and, if future knowers were eliminated, then (against his position) nothing knowable could subsist as such. (And, again, the same, mutatis mutandis, for the pair perception/perceptible.)[22]

In face of what has been said, it seems clear that neither of these two arguments can be accepted; nor, therefore, can we consider it proved by them that, if knowledge and perception ceased altogether to exist, the knowable and perceptible would continue to exist, whereas the converse is not true. To this extent, neither of these arguments substantiates any failure of reciprocation as to implication of existence, and, consequently, of natural simultaneity, on the part of these two pairs of relatives.

What has just been said helps us to reply to someone who would argue that the above line of reasoning could also be applied, with the necessary adaptations, to *V B*. Indeed, the arguer could maintain that this latter argument assumes that, although perception only appears with the emergence of animals, "the perceptible exists even before perception exists", but that this does not seem to be true for the reasons given. However, upon reflection, it is easy to conclude that there is a relevant difference in relation to the two arguments that we have just analysed. It is one thing to have a world deprived of any possible knowledge and perception, as is supposed in these two arguments from the moment animals were eliminated; it is another thing to have a world where such deprivation is to be overcome at some point in time, as assumed in *V B*. Now, if it is true that, on that line of reasoning, knowable and perceptible things could not exist, as such, in a world deprived of subjects capable of knowledge and perception, nothing hinders their existence in a world that, despite being currently deprived of them, will in the future harbour beings that can know and perceive.

But does this mean that argument *V B* (and argument *IV A*, which is a kind of counterpart to it) is problem-free? Far from it. The most devastating problem that afflicts them has to do with the interpretation of the problematic pairs in light of RRIE. Recall that, in order to accommodate Aristotle's views that some relatives do not reciprocate as to implication of existence, this rule must be read as making a narrower and more robust requirement than the ones made by both RC and RR, since, according to those views, all relatives are subject to the latter, but not all are subject to the former.[23] It is now time to assess whether such a reading is legitimate. A simple reflection allows us to conclude that it is not. And the reason is that, no matter what Aristotle would have to say about it, from the correlativity and reciprocity of these relatives, *we can infer their reciprocation as to implication of existence*. Consider again RC: every relative has a correlative, in relation to which it is said to be what it is. Now, this clearly entails that every time there is a relative, there is its correlative, and, by RR, vice versa; and it also entails that every time the latter is wanting, so it is the former, and, by RR, vice versa. However, *this is precisely what RRIE claims*. According to the reformulated version of the rule, if a relative comes to be *R* of its correlative, the latter comes to be *R'* of the former, and vice versa; and if a relative ceases to be *R* of its correlative, the latter ceases to be *R'* of the former, and vice versa. It is therefore easy to see that nothing could at the same time satisfy both RC and RR and not satisfy RRIE. Now, the same applies in the cases of the problematic pairs too. In fact, they also abide by RRIE, since, if one relative begins to exist, that is, to be a relative, the other also begins to exist, that is, to be its correlative, and vice versa; and if one ceases to exist, that is, to be a relative, the other also ceases to exist, that is, to be its correlative, and vice versa. The situation of the problematic pairs can, in this respect, be viewed in exactly the same way as the one of the master whose slave has died and, in general, as every case where the temporal asymmetry involves the present and the past rather than the present and the future, a situation in which one of the correlates is no more, but the relatives subsist: in fact, because the relatives persist, the correlativity also persists; and, *as long as* the correlativity persists, the two relatives exist, that is, are relative (which we can now see to be a simple tautology). Now, if the situation is analogous, RC, reinforced by RR, entails reciprocation as to implication of existence in the case of the problematic pairs as well. For example, if something is knowable, then, by RC, it is knowable by a certain knowledge, which exists as knowledge of that knowable (that is, simply as its correlative); if a knowable exists as such, then the knowledge by which it is said to be knowable also exists, even if the subject in which this knowledge inheres does not yet exist. Analogously with the cases of temporal asymmetry involving the present and the past, in cases such as the problematic ones, in which the temporal asymmetry involves the present and the future, the situation could then be described as follows: one of the correlates does not yet exist, but either correlative can only exist as long as both of them exist. It is therefore never the case that a knowable begins to exist as knowable by a certain knowledge before that knowledge begins to exist as knowledge of that knowable (and, uncontroversially, vice versa), nor that some knowledge ceases to exist as knowledge of a certain knowable before that knowable ceases to exist as knowable by that knowledge (and, uncontroversially, vice versa).

So, the relevant consequence here is that *all* relatives reciprocate as to implication of existence, insofar as (*contra* Aristotle) reciprocation as to implication of existence is inferred from the conjunction of the correlativity and the reciprocity of relatives, which, as we have seen, are definitional to them. To this extent, if Aristotle wanted to abdicate the natural simultaneity of the problematic pairs based on their not satisfying RRIE, he would also have to abdicate their relativity and, therefore, expel them from the category of relatives. But it seems evident that Aristotle would not be willing to take this step,[24] so he would have to accept that they too satisfy RRIE, and therefore – since there does not seem to be, in this case, any causal connection involved – that they too are naturally simultaneous.[25]

Notes

1 Note the high concentration of occurrences of the verb δοκέω in the excerpt: no less than 5, in only 37 Bekker lines.

2 As we have seen, Aristotle adds that only "in few cases, if any, could one find knowledge coming into existence at the same time as what is knowable" (7b25–27). Ancient commentators valued this observation, seeking to justify it in ingenious ways: see, in particular, Porphyry, *In Cat.* 121.4–15 Busse, and Simplicius, *In Cat.* 191.7–15 Kalbfleisch.

3 The example of the squaring of the circle, which is given to illustrate this last statement, although it does illustrate it, would better come, as it is formulated, in the wake of the first argument. Philoponus seems to realise this (*In Cat.* 121.5–8 Busse), but what he emphasises is that this example has more to do with temporal priority than with natural priority (an issue to which I will return in a moment).

4 Given the context, it is likely that ζῷον, translated in the text as "animal", means here, in fact, living being, specifically referring to mortal and immortal rational living beings. Bodéüs 2001: 126n3 finds it strange that Aristotle speaks of animal and not man, since "il suffisait d'envisager la disparition de l'espèce pour formuler l'argument". The reason may be the one given.

5 Contrary to what occurs in *IV C*, ζῷον seems here to simply mean animal. Note, by the way, that it is the possession of perception that defines what it is to be an animal for Aristotle: cf. *APo.* II 19, 99b34–35; *De an.* II 2, 413b1–4; III 3, 427b6–8; III 11, 434a5–7; III 12, 434a30–b8; *Sens.* 1, 436b8–13; *SomnVig.* 1, 454b25; *Juv.* 1, 467b23–25; 3, 469a19–20; 4, 469b4–5; *PA* II 5, 651b4–5; II 8, 653b23–24; *IA* 4, 705b10; *GA* I 23, 731a30–b5; II 1, 732a12–13; *Metaph.* I 1, 980a27–28; *EN* IX 9, 1170a16.

6 Here too, ζῷον seems to mean simply animal.

7 This is the case with Ammonius, *In Cat.* 75.6–9 Busse; Philoponus, *In Cat.* 120.3–6 Busse; Simplicius, *In Cat.* 193.17–32 Kalbfleisch; Olympiodorus,

In Cat. 108.22–109.12 Busse; Elias, 213.26–215.17 Busse; cf. Averroes, *Middle Commentary* §58. In modern times, Edelhoff 2020: 42 and 48–49 also adheres to this interpretation.

8 Almost inevitably, considering the original temporal connotation of the terms involved, such as πρότερον, ὕστερον, ἅμα, etc. – to which, however, Aristotle explicitly reserves non-temporal uses, as testified by *Cat.* 12 and 13.

9 See above, chapter 3.3.

10 I am obviously using "asynchrony" here in an atemporal sense. Again, given the original temporal meaning of expressions like "simultaneity", "priority", "synchrony", "asynchrony", it is almost impossible to avoid some degree of ambiguity when these expressions are being non-temporally construed, as is here the case, following Aristotle's own stipulations.

11 Aristotle himself is perfectly aware of the distinction between the meanings of the last term, "perceptible" and "perceived": see *De an.* III 2, 426a20–26 (and cf. *Metaph.* IX 6, 1048b13–14).

12 The recognition of such simultaneity in the case of perception and the perceived is, furthermore, explicitly assumed at *De an.* III 2, 425b26–426a1 and 426a15–19. More on the causal nexus issue later (see 5.3).

13 See, for example: Zucca 2011: 196; Santos 2016: 89n115; Erismann 2016: 407; and cf. also: Ackrill 1963: 100–101; Caujolle-Zaslawsky 1980: 181–182; Oehler 1984: 247; Bodéüs 2001: 125n4.

14 However, as we shall see later (Chapter 5.3), it is not implausible that this was one of the points that, in the homologous chapter of *Cat.* 7 in the *Metaphysics* (V 15), Aristotle decided to correct in his early views on relatives.

15 Mendelsohn 2019: 47–48 also notices that Aristotle uses "knowable" in this text "in the sense of an object that corresponds to a *that* clause in English, rather than in the sense that corresponds to a name or a definite description" (48) and notes that "this fits with Aristotle's usage in the *Posterior Analytics*" (*ibid.*), also stressing the importance of the example of the squaring of the circle. In the same direction, see Edelhoff 2020: 42n76; and, in the opposite direction, Hood 2004: 35.

16 See below, Chapter 5.1.

17 We have already been through these issues more than once: see above, 1.2, 2.1, and especially 2.3 and 3.3. Yet, it could be objected at this point that Aristotle asserts in the chapter on quality that species of knowledge, like grammar or music (his examples), are not relatives, but qualities, unlike their genus (*Cat.* 8, 11a20–36); therefore – the objection would go – one might presume that the same applies to even further specified levels of knowledge, and eminently to particular pieces of knowledge. In short, when you consider specific or particular forms of knowledge, you don't

get relatives, but qualities. I believe that the objection rests on a hasty interpretation of the text. In *Cat.* 8, Aristotle begins by mentioning, among the various types of qualities, states (ἕξεις) and conditions (διάθεσεις) and by giving the "branches of knowledge" (αἵ ἐπιστῆμαι) as examples of states (8b26–35). What does he mean by saying that branches of knowledge, that is, scientific disciplines such as the two previously indicated, are states? What he means, I assume, is that those who have come to possess the body of knowledge that is encapsulated in them have acquired an inherent qualification that can be used whenever needed: for instance, when one needs to talk or to play an instrument. These ἐπιστῆμαι have become an ingrained stable disposition within the subject. Now, as states, thus understood, the ἐπιστῆμαι are not relatives, for they are not relative to anything; indeed, they are qualifications of the person who possesses them. However, this remark concerns the grammatical or musical bodies of knowledge embedded in someone. What about the actual grammatical or musical knowledge as exercised by someone – in order, for example, to acquire more knowledge or to simply contemplate the knowledge already acquired? When you consider the latter, you get specific forms of knowledge that are not qualifications, but relatives. To phrase it in plainer terms: grammar and music are not relatives, for, as Aristotle's puts it, they are not *of* something; however, *active* grammatical and musical knowledge *are* relatives, since they are necessarily relative to some knowable grammatical item and to some knowable musical item, respectively. So, the same goes with *this* grammatical knowledge and *this* musical knowledge: they are both relative, insofar as they are, respectively, of *this* grammatical knowable and of *this* musical knowable. Therefore, against the objection, Aristotle's position in *Cat.* 8, 11a20–36, is perfectly consistent with specific and indeed particular relative knowledge.

18 Note that it is not appropriate to appeal here to the notion of temporally asymmetrical relation, saying that the relation between the knowable *x* and knowledge of *x* remains even after the latter's subject of inherence has ceased to exist. For, in this case, the conclusion would be that the two relatives *are* naturally simultaneous, which is what was to be denied.

19 Porphyry (*In Cat.* 121.16–19 Busse), Simplicius (*In Cat.* 194.24–27 Kalbfleisch) and, above all, Boethius (*In Cat.* 233bd Migne), who says he is quoting Porphyry (certainly, in the great commentary to Gedalius – cf. Ebbesen 1990: 386 – perhaps through Iamblichus – cf. Strange 2014: 125n366) come very close to this line of reasoning. Modernly, Edelhoff 2020: 44 (and n87) and 48n94 takes a similar path. Porphyry and Simplicius add, however, another line of reasoning, which is more debatable: even if the animals that know and perceive were eliminated, the knowledge that the universal intelligence has of all things and the perception "universally present in the life of the cosmos" would still exist (I am merging Porphyry 120.33–121.3 with Simplicius 194.19–24).

20 Cf. Mesquita 2018: 465–466. In the same vein of the objection, see Caston 2018: 41.

21 See above, Chapter 2.4.

22 A question that could be raised at this point is whether the said conditions that govern temporally asymmetrical relations involving the future commit Aristotle to (some limited form of) the principle of plenitude. I cannot engage in a detailed discussion of this question here, but I wish to emphasise that, either way, the answer to it does not affect my point. Suppose that these conditions do commit him to this principle. Then, since a case can be made that he strongly rejects it in *Metaph.* IX 3 (and already at *Int.* 9, 19a7–22), this would be an argument for the conclusion that Aristotle evolved in his philosophical views on the problematic pairs, that he began by wrongly advocating the theses that we see him embracing in *Cat.* 7 only to later abandon them, and perhaps even (as I will suggest may be the case in Chapter 5.3) to implicitly correct them in *Metaph.* V 15. Of course, this being so, Aristotle's mature views on this matter would have entailed the restriction of temporally asymmetrical relations to those that associate past and present correlates and the rejection of those associating present and future ones. However, I am far from sure that those conditions really commit him to any form of the principle of plenitude. They would in fact commit him to a limited version of this principle if they implied that something could only be *knowable* now if at some point in the future it would become *known*. But this is *not* what temporally asymmetrical relations involving the future imply. What these relations imply is rather that something can only be knowable now if sometime in the future there will be someone by which it *could* be known, regardless of whether or not it will actually become known. The point here is that, when relatives like knowable or perceptible are at stake, it is not necessary for their correlatives to be *currently* available in the world, provided that such correlatives *will come to be available* at some point in the future. But the correlative of a present knowable thing for which there isn't any available knowledge yet is the prospective knowledge by which it will be *knowable*, not the one by which it will be *known*. In other words, what such a knowable has as its correlative is simply the possible future knowledge in relation to which it is said to be just what it is, namely, *knowable*. For this is exactly what is required by the rule of correlativity of relatives. However, taking into account the integration of this type of relation within the framework of the ontological square, for a future knowledge to be possible there must be in the future some *actual* knower; and, generally speaking, for the wanting correlative of some relative to become available in the future, there must in the future be an actual appropriate relatum as its subject of inherence. An example may be of some help here. Considering the Earth's actual history, *was* the theorem of Pythagoras knowable in the times of the dinosaurs? In

Aristotelian terms, as I construe them, no doubt it was. Why so? Because at one point in that history there will come the moment when some knowledgeable subject by whom the theorem is knowable comes about – and the fact that, in the actual course of that history, it has contingently become known is totally beside the point. The theorem could have remained forever unknown without undermining the fact that it was already knowable in the times of dinosaurs, because the only reason why it *was* already knowable is that in the future there will be a time when someone *can* know it. I am strongly inclined to favour this latter answer, both because of the merit of the argument and because it additionally offers the non-negligible advantage over the former of permitting us to keep in place the very concept of temporally asymmetrical relations involving the future.

23 See above, Chapter 3.3.

24 The impressive number of times that Aristotle uses these pairs as an example of relatives (see, above, note 25 in Chapter 1) is an obvious sign of this.

25 My assessment of arguments *IV A* and *V B* and the conclusions I draw from them are similar to the interpretation proposed by Duncombe 2020: 110–112 for the entire Aristotelian position on the natural simultaneity of relatives. From this assessment results, for the both of us, the confirmation that, correctly understood, RRIE is, in fact, a mere consequence of RC (combined with RR, it should be added), so that all relatives satisfy both rules. The difference between our two interpretations is that Duncombe's presupposes that the Aristotelian analysis is itself aware of this consequence, while, on my interpretation, not only is it not, but it is the fact that it is not that is at the root of the unsoundness of those two arguments.

5 Aftermath and Second Thoughts

5.1 Unravelling Aristotle's Train of Thought in *Cat.* 7

Considering what has been said, a conclusion seems to impose itself: in what regards the problematic pairs, Aristotle appears to be quite simply mistaken.[1] It is tempting to ask what led him astray. One explanation was long ago set forth. Aristotle's reasoning seems to be undermined by not making a necessary and important distinction: the distinction between things themselves and things *qua* knowable, for example between the theorem of Pythagoras and the theorem as a possible object of knowledge. Now, the two are not the same and must therefore not be confused: things as such are independent of and, in principle, temporally prior to knowledge, of which they are not correlative; it is only insofar as they are knowable by some possible knowledge, that is to say, it is only insofar as they bear the specific property of being knowable, that they become relative to such knowledge and reciprocate with it as to implication of existence. One thing is the theorem of Pythagoras in itself, namely, as a mathematical truth, which is independent, not correlative of and, in principle, temporally prior to any possible knowledge of it; quite another thing is the theorem as an object of some possible knowledge, of which it is correlative. The theorem of Pythagoras would always be a mathematical truth regardless of it coming to be known at one point in time or remaining forever unknown. It is this kind of fact that Aristotle has in mind when he insists that "the knowable" – by which he means in fact the thing itself – is, as a general rule, prior to knowledge (remember the example of the squaring of the circle); however, it is not as a mathematical truth that the theorem of Pythagoras is a relative, but insofar as it bears the property of being knowable by some possible knowledge,

DOI: 10.4324/9781003563266-5

which is its correlative. Now, although the theorem of Pythagoras as a mathematical truth is, in principle, temporally prior to any possible knowledge of it, yet, *as knowable*, it reciprocates as to implication of existence, and indeed is naturally simultaneous, with the possible knowledge by which it is said to be knowable.

The same goes, of course, for the perception/perceptible pair. The word "thing" is, however, a dangerously ambiguous one and this ambiguity may be specially damaging in the case of this latter pair. So, let me get this straight. When applied to the pair perceptible/perception, the word "thing" I used earlier (and will be using in what follows) does not stand just for objects as such, but specifically for their perceptible qualities as well. What I mean is not only that Aristotle overlooks or disregards the difference between, say, an object that is white, like this sheet of paper, which, under appropriate conditions, is perceptible as white, and that object qua perceptible. He probably does this too, but this is not half as harmful as overlooking or disregarding the difference between the object's property itself, say, white, and such property as perceptible.[2] Now, in his treatment of the problematic pairs, Aristotle seems indeed to be implicitly conflating properties like white, warm, sweet, and moisty, which *are*, under appropriate conditions, perceptible, with white, warm, sweet, and moisty *as* perceptible, that is, as possible objects of perception. However, the two are not to be confused: as such, properties like those are independent of and, in principle, temporally prior to perception, of which they are not correlative; it is only insofar as they *can be perceived* by someone capable of perceiving them, that is to say, it is only insofar as they themselves bear this additional property, that they are relative to perception and reciprocate with it as to implication of existence.

In short, then, the temporal priority of things that are, from the appropriate point of view, relative to other things is fully compatible with natural simultaneity of such things *as relatives*, or, more accurately put, with natural simultaneity of the relatives they instantiate; and it is, of course, only the latter that counts for the conceptual analysis of the relatives. The neglect of this distinction is, for example, amply conspicuous in arguments *IV C* and *V A*. Ancient commentators were well aware of this, even when they chose, as is the case with Porphyry, to avoid attributing the neglect to Aristotle himself. Indeed, the interpretation generally advocated by them, which is offered *en bloc* for Aristotle's thesis and, as a rule, without distinguishing the arguments that support it, contrary to what was done in the previous chapter, is essentially based on the aforementioned distinction, namely between the thing as such and the thing as knowable or perceptible, to which they typically associate another distinction: the distinction between the relations considered in potentiality and in actuality. Thus, they argue, if something is now a ἐπιστητόν and there is not yet something that is its respective ἐπιστήμη, then the correlatives are the ἐπιστητόν in potentiality (the knowable) and ἐπιστήμη in potentiality; if something is now ἐπιστήμη of a certain ἐπιστητόν, then the correlatives are the ἐπιστητόν in actuality (the known) and ἐπιστήμη in actuality. (And the same, again, for the relation αἴσθησις and αἰσθητόν.)[3] The inference they intend to draw is, of course, that the correlativity is preserved in all cases and, with it, the reciprocation as to implication of existence (which they hastily call "natural simultaneity").

Interestingly enough, a passage from the *Metaphysics* seems to surprise Aristotle as if trying to correct his previous precipitancy – of which, therefore, it would be necessary to suppose that he had at some point become aware. It is the following passage:

> In general, if indeed only the perceptible exists, nothing would exist unless animate things existed, since there would be no perception. Now that neither perceptibles (τὰ αἰσθητά) nor perceptions (τὰ αἰσθήματα) would exist is presumably true (since this is a way of the perceiver's being affected), but that the underlying subjects (τὰ ὑποκείμενα) that produce perception would not exist even without perception is impossible. For perception is certainly not perception of itself, but there is also some other thing beyond the perception, which is necessarily prior to the perception. For what moves something is prior in nature to what is moved, and even if they are said to be with reference to each other, this is no less so.[4]

Indeed, it is at least possible to interpret this passage as distinguishing – correctly – between the thing as perceptible and the thing as such (in its own terms, between the perceptible and the subject that produces the perception). Now, in doing so, it becomes possible to recognise – once again, correctly – that the thing as such is prior to perception (1010b36–1011a2), but that the thing as perceptible is not (1010b31–33).

Should this interpretation of the passage be admitted, then one would expect that the chapter of the *Metaphysics* that Aristotle dedicates to relatives (V 15), and which is the counterpart of chapter 7 of the *Categories*, would show a considerable departure from this latter text, especially regarding the understanding of the relatives involved in the problematic pairs and the type of priority/posteriority or simultaneity relations that obtain between them. And, conversely, if such a departure were to be verified, this would constitute a powerful argument not only in favour of the proposed reading of the quoted passage but, in general, in favour of the interpretation I advanced for the issue of natural simultaneity of relatives in the *Categories*.

5.2 Relatives in *Metaph.* V 15

That the aforementioned chapter of the *Metaphysics* adopts a completely different perspective from that adopted in chapter 7 of the *Categories* on relatives, and that any reference to most of the themes dealt with in the latter is completely absent in the former, namely the issue of natural simultaneity, is evident and indisputable. But it could be argued that the way in which the class of relatives that integrates the problematic pairs is approached in *Metaph.* V 15 – and, from the outset, the fact that it is there seen as a particular class of relatives – seems to substantiate a continuity in the attribution of a status of exceptionality to those pairs, even perhaps providing a means of understanding the one that is ascribed to them in *Cat.* 7. Indeed, it is commonly accepted that Aristotle, in *Metaph.* V 15, incorporates the problematic pairs into a separate class of relatives and that, therefore, he finds in them, and in general in the members of this class, something distinctive. A different question, however, is whether what is distinctive about them is in line with or even confirms the solution (always tentatively) offered by Aristotle for the natural simultaneity of these pairs in *Cat.* 7, or whether, on the contrary, it is entirely independent of, or even contradictory to, this solution. To solve the problem, we have to resort to the text.

The angle of approach followed by Aristotle in the treatment of relatives in *Metaph.* V 15 and the principle of organisation that he there proposes for them are very different from those we saw applied in *Cat.* 7. In the *Metaphysics*, relatives are essentially divided into two groups, the first of which is in turn subdivided into two others. The first main group brings together those relatives that are "said to be just what they are of another thing" (1021a28).[5] In this group, two subgroups are distinguished: on the one hand, numerical relatives, that is, relatives that are constituted as such by a numerical relation, definite or indefinite, such as double and half, triple and third, of several times greater and several times smaller, equal, similar, same; on the other hand, relatives regarding a capacity, that is, relatives that are constituted as such by the existence of a capacity over others and, conversely, of the respective receptivity, as well as by their actualisations, such as being able to heat and being able to be heated, to heat and to be heated, to be able to cut and to be able to be cut, to cut and to be cut, or father and son. The second main group is that of relatives in which *another thing*, not themselves, is said to be what it is in relation to them (1021a29–30), as is the case with the measurable and measure, the knowable and knowledge, the perceptible and perception, the thinkable and thought. For, in each of these pairs, the first member is only said to be a relative because the second is *relative to it*, in the sense that it is the latter that constitutes the relation with the former: measure makes something measurable, knowledge makes something knowable, thought makes something thinkable, etc. Such relatives can, therefore, justifiably be described as *intentional*, insofar as the relation results entirely from the intentionality of one of the relatives (the original or constitutive relative, such as knowledge or thought) over the other (the subordinate relative, e.g., the knowable or the thinkable).[6] Thus, if we now ignore the distinction between the two main groups (as Aristotle himself initially does), we can say that three types of relatives are enumerated here: (1) relatives correlated by a numerical relation; (2) relatives correlated by the capacity of an agent over a patient and the patient's receptivity towards the former, or by their respective actualisations; and (3) intentional relatives.[7] Now, the point which seems to lie latent under Aristotle's description, though never made explicit, is that the first two types of relative *both* satisfy the first definition of *Cat.* 7 (and therefore are both said to be just what they are of their correlative), whereas, in the case of relatives of the third type, *only one of them* is relative in this sense, that is, is said to be just what it is of its correlative, namely when it intentionally constitutes the relation itself.

5.3 Contrasting *Cat.* 7 with *Metaph.* V 15

It would be tempting to use this purported specificity of intentional relatives to construe the failure of natural simultaneity that Aristotle attributes to the problematic pairs in *Cat.* 7. The basic idea would be that the members of these pairs are not simultaneous by nature, but one of them is by nature prior to the other, because it is the latter (knowledge or perception) that, when emerging, constitutes the relation with the former (the knowable or the perceptible), which must therefore *already* be present.[8]

I have many doubts that this path leads anywhere, for several reasons, of which I will highlight the following two. The first reason is that the very distinction drawn in *Metaph.* V 15 between the two main groups of relatives seems to me, as it is formulated, artificial and highly unsatisfactory. In Aristotle's words, it is knowledge that is relative to the knowable and not the other way around, because it is knowledge that is said to be just what it is of the knowable, or relative to it. But is it not also true that, *qua knowable*, the knowable is said to be just what it is of knowledge, or relative to knowledge? What could be said truly is that it is *originally* knowledge that is relative to the knowable, that is to say, that it is knowledge that constitutes the relation through which the knowable becomes such; but, as soon as the relation is established, both knowledge is relative to the knowable and said to be just what it is of it *and* the knowable is relative to knowledge and said to be just what it is of it. That is to say, once the relation is established, the definition of the *Categories* applies equally to the two relatives – which would be expected, if they really are relatives and if the definition applies to all relatives, as Aristotle maintains. Here, again, we face the same misstep derived from not distinguishing between the thing as such and the thing as knowable, that is, between the thing *that was already there before* and the thing *made knowable* by the intentional relation, which only begins to exist with the relation itself.[9]

The second reason is as follows. So far, I have followed the usual translation of this passage, which translates μετρητόν as "measurable", ἐπιστητόν as "knowable", αἰσθητόν as "perceptible" and διανοητόν as "thinkable". However, the context seems to require that these words be translated rather as "measured", "known", "perceived" and "thought", respectively. Indeed, in 1021a31 it is said that διανοητόν "signifies that *there is* thought of it" (τό τε γὰρ διανοητὸν σημαίνει ὅτι ἔστιν αὐτοῦ διάνοια).[10] This makes it plausible that the word διανοητόν is being used here in the sense of "thought", not of "thinkable". Now, since its inclusion in the second main group follows the same rule that applies to the other pairs, μετρητόν and μέτρον, ἐπιστητόν and ἐπιστήμη, αἰσθητόν and αἴσθησις, the same reading must, by analogy, be applied to the first members of each one.[11] However, this being the case, this text and that of *Cat.* 7 are not, after all, talking about the same pairs of relatives, so what is said in the former cannot serve to illuminate what is said in the latter, namely the failure of natural simultaneity of the problematic pairs.

Let us admit, however, that it is in fact the measurable, the knowable, the perceptible, the thinkable (and not the measured, the known, the perceived, the thought) that Aristotle wants to consider here and, therefore, that, presumably, the intention behind the line in 1021a31 would be better captured in Reeve's translation: "signifies that there *can be* a thought of it". If so, this reading, far from supporting and strengthening Aristotle's position on the problematic pairs in *Cat.* 7, provides a new, and quite powerful, argument *against* that position. In fact, if it is knowledge that makes a knowable to be knowable and perception that makes a perceptible to be perceptible, then *there can be no* knowables before knowledge, nor perceptibles before perception. There certainly are things that *will become* knowable or perceptible. But, again, things as such and things as knowable or perceptible must not be confounded. Furthermore, if this were the case, the theory of intentional relatives developed by Aristotle in this text would be structurally committed to the simultaneity – in this case, both natural and temporal – of these relatives and, therefore, to the simultaneity of the problematic pairs. And, since it is hardly credible that Aristotle would not be aware of this fact, this would then be a reason to see in this theory the purpose of correcting the mistaken theses that he had proposed in this regard in *Cat.* 7. And this, as was said above, would constitute a strong additional independent corroboration of the interpretation I have been defending.

There would certainly be an audacious way of avoiding admitting, in this context, the natural simultaneity of the problematic pairs: namely, to hold that, in each of them, one of the relatives, the one which intentionally constitutes the relation, is, for that reason, the cause of the existence of the other. However, not only is it not very clear under what kind of cause this intentional cause would fall within the framework of the Aristotelian theory of causality (if a strong, proper sense is to be given to the word "cause"), but the fact is that Aristotle does not say anything that leads us in that direction.

Alternatively, one could invoke the passage of *Metaph.* IV 5 previously quoted and argue that the very notion of "underlying subjects that *produce* perception" (τὰ ὑποκείμενα ἃ ποιεῖ τὴν αἴσθησιν: 1010b33–34), and the final remark that "what moves something is prior in nature to what is moved, and even if they are said to be with reference to each other, this is no less so" (1010b37–1011a2), invites the reader to conclude that there is in fact a causal relation linking the members of at least this problematic pair – one that, however, runs in the opposite direction, namely from perceptible things to perception.[12] It is true that such a reading is consistent with Aristotle's theory of perception in the *De anima* and supported by a number of formal proclamations by Aristotle.[13] It is however open to debate whether these causes of perception should be thought of as the things as such or the things qua perceptible, in the sense in which we introduced this distinction above. Now, in addition to the fact that the most natural reading of the texts points to the former, Aristotle's analysis of intentional relatives in *Metaph.* V 15 seems hardly compatible with the latter, which is the one required for disproving the natural simultaneity of the two relatives as such. More to the point, a strong case can be made that, in the terms of that theory, such causes are causes of the perceptual contents, not causes of the fact of there being perception, which ultimately depends on natural capacities of animals' bodies and souls. Yet, the causal condition of natural simultaneity concerns the cause *of existence.*[14] Furthermore, how would this model of causality apply to the knowledge/knowable pair? Even if we concede that Aristotle conceives perceptibles as somehow productive of perception – for instance, as unactualised capacities or powers to produce perception, following Caston 2018 – it seems to be lacking any textual support or philosophical motivation to ascribe him the view that knowables are unactualised capacities or powers to produce knowledge, or as productive of knowledge in any analogous manner. Causality thought of in this way does not appear, therefore, to qualify as a *general* explanation for an alleged failure of natural simultaneity of the problematic pairs.

Be that as it may, even if it could be established that Aristotle eventually came to adopt either one of these causal hypotheses in any suitable sense, this would show him, again, moving away from the views taken in this regard in *Cat.* 7 and seeking to correct them, since no hint in any of these directions can be found in this chapter. And, especially in the case of the first hypothesis, even so the *Metaphysics* chapter on relatives would have to be seen as an exercise in correcting the homologous chapter of the *Categories*, without anything in it validating the positions taken in the latter on the alleged exceptionality of the problematic pairs.

Notes

1 To mitigate the force of this conclusion, account must be taken of the particular frequency with which Aristotle uses in this section of the text expressions of doubt, suggesting that he is not entirely sure of the theses he is advancing.

2 I am working on the assumption that Aristotle's adopts a realistic approach to sensible properties. For a recent defence of this point of view – which, as will become clear in a moment (see below, 5.3), I may not be able to unreservedly accept in all its details – see Caston 2018. However, we don't need to make such a huge theoretical investment here, if we simply understand "white" (or any other sensible property "*s*") as designating the property that some perceptual subject, namely a standard human perceiver, sees as white (or that such a subject perceives as *s*).

3 See, with occasional nuances in formulation and modes of presentation: Porphyry, *In Cat.* 120.23–33 Busse; Ammonius, *In Cat.* 76.10–77.2 Busse; Philoponus, *In Cat.* 122.23–124.14 Busse; Simplicius, *In Cat.* 193.33–194.27 and 196.24–33 Kalbfleisch; Olympiodorus, *In Cat.* 109.13–19 Busse; Elias, *In Cat.* 213.26–215.10 Busse. Note that this interpretation anticipates the aforementioned one (see note 13 in chapter 4 and the text it refers to), according to which the correct correlates are knowledge/known and perception/perceived, although these commentators consider that the correlations between knowable and potential knowledge and between perceptible and potential perception are equally correct. In modern times, the first distinction referred to in the text was also hinted at by Cavarnos 1975: 48 and Ganson 1997: 267n9; in antiquity, see Sergius of Reshaina, *In Cat.* 340–342 Arzhanov (cf. 346).

4 *Metaph.* IV 5, 1010b30–1011a2; Reeve's translation.

5 Aristotle returns here to the first definition of relatives from *Cat.* 7 (6a36–37).

6 Aristotle mentions again this second group of relatives, in identical terms, in *Metaph.* X 6, 1056b32–1057a1.

7 Kirwan 1993: 164–165 draws attention to the fact that this tripartite classification of the relatives does not seem to encompass all the relatives recognised by Aristotle in *Cat.* 7, such as large/small or master/slave. Complementarily, Harari 2011: 528 notes that the list of examples offered by Aristotle at the beginning of *Cat.* 7 includes examples of all three classes of relatives distinguished in *Metaph.* V 15; however, the impact of this observation is somewhat limited if we consider that the sequence observed by Aristotle in the indication of relatives in the *Categories* does not respect the division into the three kinds recognised in the *Metaphysics*. The issue of the relationship between the two descriptions of relatives has given rise to much controversy. Those who defend the harmony of

the two descriptions include, for instance: Morales 1994: 255; Bodéüs 2001: XLVIIn3; Harari 2011: 528; Bodéüs/Stevens 2014: 161; Duncombe 2020: 141–160. Those who defend their difference and the evolution from one to the other include: Kirwan 1993: 164; Gottlieb 1993: 107–109; Hood 2004: 55, 82–84. Echoes, partial and incomplete, of this tripartite classification of relatives can be found in: *Ph.* III 1, 200b26–32; *Metaph.* X 6, 1056b32–1057a1.

8 Mendelsohn's analysis 2019: 46–47, although without expressly referring to the issue of simultaneity, goes strongly in this direction.

9 This misstep is unwittingly but significantly reflected in the following comment by Ross: "At the bottom of Aristotle's thought, though not very satisfactorily expressed, is the conviction that knowledge and perception are relative to reality in a way in which reality is not relative to them" (1924: 331).

10 So Ross, Rolfe, Tredennick, Kirwan, Yebra, Calvo, Sachs, Duminil/Jaulin and Bodéüs/Stevens. Reeve opts instead for: "signifies that there can be a thought of it" (in the same vein, see also Hood 2004: 65–68). However, though it is evidently true that the verb εἰμί can have the sense of being possible, it seems rather dubious to me that it can have the sense of being possible that *it exists*; see also on this Duncombe 2020: 152–153.

11 Although translators, including those mentioned in the previous note, generally adopt the other translation here.

12 See Caston 2018 for a recent defence of this view.

13 See *Sens.* 2, 438b22–23; 3, 439a16–17; 4, 442b22–23; 6, 445b4–8; and maybe *Mete.* IV 8, 384b34–385a4e.

14 Consider again *Cat.* 13, 14b27–29: φύσει δὲ ἅμα ὅσα ἀντιστρέφει μὲν κατὰ τὴν τοῦ εἶναι ἀκολούθησιν, μηδαμῶς δὲ *αἴτιον θάτερον θατέρῳ τοῦ εἶναί* ἐστιν.

6 Conclusion

Let us briefly recall the main itinerary that has been followed throughout this book. After having pointed out its main target, namely the issue of the natural simultaneity of relatives as discussed by Aristotle in *Cat.* 7, 7b15–8a12, a general description of the whole chapter was given, highlighting the aspects most relevant to the analysis of this issue, to the detriment of others that have received more attention in modern commentary. Against this background, the problem to be addressed, namely Aristotle's position regarding two pairs of relatives he sees as failures of natural simultaneity (the "problematic pairs", knowledge/knowable and perception/perceptible), was described in detail.

Next, the notion of relatives in Aristotle's *Categories* was examined, and an interpretation of how this notion should be understood in the framework of the Aristotelian metaphysics underlying this treatise was offered. We saw then that the ontological square set forth in *Cat.* 2 presents serious challenges to the relatives, specifically in cases where relative and correlative are not temporarily simultaneous, that is to say, in cases where their respective subjects of inherence (the relatum and the correlate) exist in partially different times. In this context, the notion of temporally asymmetrical relations was advanced as a solution to those challenges. According to this notion, although the two relata exist in partially different times, the relation itself (hence the correlativity and the reciprocity), if it is not interrupted, subsists for as long as any of them exists from the moment the relation was established. In cases such as these, thus, relatives may have correlatives for which there is currently no subject of inherence. This notion was then applied to the problematic pairs, in which the

DOI: 10.4324/9781003563266-6

existence of the correlation requires that one of the relata, although currently missing, will eventually be there in the future.

The following chapter was devoted to the concept of natural simultaneity, in the sense relevant to the relatives. We saw that this notion arguably corresponds to the second sense of simultaneity presented by Aristotle in *Cat.* 13 and that it therefore contains two conditions: reciprocation as to implication of existence and the causal condition. A reconstruction of the former was offered with a view to accommodate Aristotle's perspective that some relatives do not reciprocate as to implication of existence, and hence satisfy both RC and RR, but not RRIE, without thereby committing one to accept such perspective.

Chapter 4 was dedicated to presenting the text of *Cat.* 7 where the issue of the natural simultaneity of relatives is discussed by Aristotle (7b15–8a12) and to reconstruct the five arguments he offers in favour of the thesis of the exceptional character of the problematic pairs in this regard. Each of these arguments was then thoroughly analysed and discussed, and the conclusion was reached that, by virtue of the principles to which Aristotle is committed, none of them succeeds in proving this thesis.

Finally, in Chapter 5, a tentative reconstruction of the line of reasoning that may have led Aristotle to embrace this thesis was outlined, after which a comparison of *Cat.* 7 with its counterpart in the *Metaphysics* (V 15) allowed us to detect what appears to be a departure, in the latter, from the perspectives adopted in the former regarding the natural simultaneity of relatives, and even encouraged us to envisage the chapter on relatives in the *Metaphysics* as if it was, in this particular point, an exercise in correcting the parallel chapter of the *Categories*.

At the end of the journey, we can therefore summarise as follows the main thread of this book and its chief conclusions:

1. By definition, every relative has a correlative, in relation to which it is said to be what it is.
2. Correlatives reciprocate and, therefore, are, in turn, said to be just what they are in relation to their relatives.
3. From these two principles, it follows that the existence of a relative implies the existence of its correlative and vice versa, so (contrary to what is said in *Cat.* 7) all relatives reciprocate as to implication of existence.

4. The problematic pairs are no exception in this respect, nor do they have anything truly problematic. In fact, one could say that they are just as simultaneous by nature as the canonical examples that Aristotle gives (the pairs double/half and master/slave), since not only do the relatives within each of those pairs reciprocate as to implication of existence, but neither of them seems to be the cause of the other's existence.
5. We are therefore forced to conclude that Aristotle was led astray on this matter. This certainly gives a special value to the doubtful expressions which, although characteristic of the chapter in general, and indeed of the treatise as a whole, recur with a particular frequency throughout the section on natural simultaneity.
6. However, from the foregoing it does not necessarily follow that all relatives are naturally simultaneous. For that, it would be necessary to exclude that some are the cause of the existence of their correlatives. But this may not be viable, because there arguably are relatives that, although reciprocating as to implication of existence with their correlatives, are, notwithstanding, the cause of their existence, as is the case, for instance, of the parent/child pair.

References

Ackrill, J.L. (1963), *Aristotle's Categories and De Interpretatione*. Oxford, Clarendon Press.

Angelelli, I. (1967), *Studies on Gottlob Frege and Traditional Philosophy*. New York, Humanities Press.

Angelelli, I. (1985), "En torno al 'cuadrado ontológico'", *Anuario Filosófico* 18: 23–32.

Arzhanov, Y. (2024), *Sergius of Reshaina. Commentary on Aristotle's Categories. Critical Edition and Translation*. Berlin – Boston, De Gruyter.

Aydin, S. (2016), *Sergius of Reshaina: Introduction to Aristotle and his Categories, Addressed to Philotheos*. Leiden, Brill.

Aydin, S. (2019), "The Remnant of a Questions and Answers Commentary on Aristotle's *Categories* in Syriac (*Vat. Syr. 586*)", *Studia graeco-arabica* 9.

Bodéüs, R. (2001), *Aristote: Catégories*. Paris, Les Belles Lettres.

Bodéüs, R., Stevens, A. (2014), *Aristote Metaphysique Livre Delta*. Paris, Vrin.

Bonelli, M. (2011), "Aristotele, *Categorie* 7, 6a36–7b14, la prima definizione dei relativi e alcune loro proprietà", *Studi sulle Categorie di Aristotele*, ed. M. Bonelli and F. G. Masi. Amsterdam, Adolf M. Hakkert: 173–190.

Bonelli, M. (2018), "Substances and Relatives in Aristotle's *Categories* (Chapter 7)", *Rivista di storia della filosofia* 3: 384–396.

Brandis, C.A. (1836), *Scholia in Aristotelem*. Berolini, Georgium Reimerum.

Brower, J.E. (2016), "Aristotelian vs. Contemporary Perspectives on Relations", *The Metaphysics of Relations*, ed. A. Marmodoro and D. Yates. New York, Oxford University Press: 36–54.

Brunschwig, J. (1967), *Topiques. I-IV*, Paris, Belles Lettres.

Busse, A. (1887), "Porphyrii *Isagoge* et in Aristotelis *Categorias* commentarium", *Commentaria in Aristotelem graeca*, IV-1. Berolini, Typis et impensis Georgii Reimeri.

Busse, A. (1895), "Ammonius in Aristotelis *Categorias* commentarius", *Commentaria in Aristotelem graeca*, IV-4. Berolini, Typis et impensis Georgii Reimeri.

Busse, A. (1898), "Philoponi (olim Ammonii) in Aristotelis *Categorias* commentarium", *Commentaria in Aristotelem graeca*, XIII-1. Berolini, Typis et impensis Georgii Reimeri.

Busse, A. (1900), "Eliae in Prophyrii *Isagogen* et Aristotelis *Categorias* commentaria", *Commentaria in Aristotelem graeca*, XVIII-1. Berolini, Typis et impensis Georgii Reimeri.

Busse, A. (1902), "Olympiodori Prolegomena et in *Categorias* commentarium", *Commentaria in Aristotelem graeca*, XII-1. Berolini, Typis et impensis Georgii Reimeri.

Butterworth, C.E. (1983), *Averroes' Middle Commentaries on Aristotle's Categories and De Interpretatione*. Princeton (NJ), Princeton University Press.

Calvo Martínez, T. (1994), *Metafísica*. Madrid, Editorial Gredos.

Caston, V. (2018), "Aristotle on the Reality of Colors and Other Perceptible Qualities", *Res Philosophica* 95: 35–68.

Caujolle-Zaslawsky, F. (1980), "Les relatifs dans les *Catégories*", *Concepts et catégories dans la pensée antique*, ed. P. Aubenque. Paris, Vrin: 167–195.

Cavarnos, C. (1975), *The Classical Theory of Relations. A Study in the Metaphysics of Plato, Aristotle, and Thomism.* Belmont (MA), Institute for Byzantine and Modem Greek Studies.

Chiaradona, R., Rashed, M. (2020), *Boéthos de Sidon – Exégète d'Aristote et philosophe*. Berlin – Boston, De Gruyter.

Cleary, J. (1988), *Aristotle on the Many Senses of Priority.* Carbondale (IL), Southern Illinois University Press.

Cohen, S.M. (2008), "Kooky Objects Revisited: Aristotle's Ontology", *Metaphilosophy* 39: 3–19.

Cohen, S.M. (2013), "Accidental Beings in Aristotle's Ontology", *Reason and Analysis in Ancient Greek Philosophy. Essays in Honor of David Keyt*, ed. G. Anagnostopoulos and F. D. Miller. Dordrecht, Springer: 231–242.

Cohen, S.M., Matthews, G.B. (2014), *Ammonius. On Aristotle's Categories*. London, Bloomsbury Publishing.

Conti, A.D. (1983), "La teoria della relazione nei commentari neoplatonici alle *Categorie* di Aristotele", *Rivista critica di storia della filosofia* 3: 259–283.

Corkum, P. (2016), "Ontological Dependence and Grounding in Aristotle", *Oxford Handbooks Online*, June 2016.

Crubellier, M. (2013), "Domestiquer l'excès de l'être. La catégorie des relatifs entre Platon et Aristote", *Quaestio* 13: 3–15.

Delcogliano, M. (2010), *Basil of Caesarea's Anti-Eunomian Theory of Names. Christian Theology and Late-Antique Philosophy in the Fourth Century Trinitarian Controversy*. Leiden – Boston, Brill.

Demetracopoulos, J.A. (1996), "Aristotle's *Categories* in the Greek and Latin Medieval Exegetical Tradition. The Case of the Argument for the

Non-Simultaneity of Relatives", *Cahiers de l'Institut du Moyen Âge grec et latin* 66: 117–134.

Duminil, M.-P., Jaulin, A. (2008), *Aristote. Métaphysique*. Paris, Flammarion.

Duncombe, M. (2015), "Aristotle's Two Accounts of Relatives in *Categories* 7", *Phronesis* 60: 436–461.

Duncombe, M. (2018), "Aristotle's *Categories* 7 Adopts Plato's View of Relativity", *Authors and Authorities in Ancient Philosophy*, ed. J. Bryan, R. Wardy and J. Warren. Cambridge, Cambridge University Press: 120–138.

Duncombe, M. (2020), *Ancient Relativity. Plato, Aristotle, Stoics, and Sceptics*. New York, Oxford University Press.

Ebbesen, S. (1990), "Boethius as an Aristotelian commentator", *Aristotle Transformed. The Ancient Commentators and Their Influence*, ed. R. Sorabji. Ithaca (NY), Cornell University Press: 373–391.

Ebbesen, S., Marenbon, J., Thom, P. (2013), *Aristotle's Categories in the Byzantine, Arabic and Latin Traditions*. Copenhagen, Det Kongelige Danske Videnskabernes Selskab.

Edelhoff, A.L. (2020), *Aristotle on Ontological Priority in the Categories*. Cambridge, Cambridge University Press.

Erismann, C. (2016), "Venerating Likeness: Byzantine Iconophile Thinkers on Aristotelian Relatives and their Simultaneity", *British Journal for the History of Philosophy* 24: 405–425.

Fleet, G. (2002), *Simplicius. On Aristotle's Categories 7–8*. London, Bloomsbury Publishing.

Gambra, J.M. (2013), "La définition des relatifs dans les *Catégories* et son emploi dans les *Topiques*", *Philosophie antique* 13: 225–242.

Ganson, T.S. (1997), "What's Wrong with the Aristotelian Theory of Sensible Qualities?", *Phronesis* 42: 263–282.

Gaskin, R. (2013), *Simplicius. On Aristotle's Categories 9–15*. London, Bloomsbury Publishing.

Georr, K. (1948), *Les Catégories d'Aristote dans leurs versions syro-arabes. Édition de textes précédée d'une étude historique et critique et suivie d'un vocabulaire technique*. Beyrouth, Institut Français de Damas.

Gerson, L.P. *et al.* (2018), *Plotinus. The Enneads*. Cambridge, Cambridge University Press.

Gottlieb, P. (1993), "Aristotle versus Protagoras on Relatives and the Objects of Perception", *Oxford Studies in Ancient Philosophy* 11: 101–119.

Gourinat, J.-B. (2013), "Relations et relatifs: les Stoïciens contre Aristote", *Quaestio* 13: 17–38.

Harari, O. (2011), "The Unity of Aristotle's Category of Relatives", *Classical Quarterly* 61: 521–537.

Hood, P. (2004), *Aristotle on the Category of Relation*. Lanham (MD), University Press of America.

Jansen, L. (2006), "Aristoteles' Kategorien des Relativen zwischen Dialektik und Ontologie", *Logical Analysis and History of Philosophy* 9: 79–104.

Jones, J.R. (1949), "Are the Qualities of Particular Things Universal or Particular?", *Philosophical Review* 58: 152–170.

Kalbfleisch, K. (1907), "Simplicii in Aristotelis *Categorias* commentarium", *Commentaria in Aristotelem graeca*, VIII. Berolini, Typis et impensis Georgii Reimeri.

Kirwan, C. (1993), *Metaphysics Books Gamma, Delta, and Epsilon*. Oxford, Clarendon Press.

Luna, C. (2013), "Boéthos de Sidon sur les relatifs", *Studia Graeco-Arabica* 3: 1–35.

Marmodoro, M., Yates, D. (2016), "Introduction", *The Metaphysics of Relations*, ed. A. Marmodoro and D. Yates. New York, Oxford University Press: 1–18.

Martin, C. (2016), "The Invention of Relations: Early Twelfth-Century Discussions of Aristotle's Account of Relatives", *British Journal for the History of Philosophy* 24: 447–467.

Mendelsohn, J. (2019), *Aristotle on the Necessity of What We Know*. PhD Dissertation, University of Chicago.

Mesquita, A.P. (2018), "Aristotle on the Nature of Time. Review of: Chelsea Harry's, *Chronos in Aristotle's Physics: On the Nature of Time*", *Ancient Philosophy* 38: 460–466.

Migne, J.-P. (1847), "Anicii Manlii Torquati Severini Boetii, In *Categorias* Aristotelis libri quatuor", *Patrologiae cursus completus: series latina*. Parisiis, Venit apud editorem: LXIV, 159–294.

Mignucci, M. (1986), "Aristotle's Definitions of Relatives in *Cat.* 7", *Phronesis* 31: 101–127.

Minio-Paluello, L. (1949), *Aristotelis: Categoriae et Liber de Interpretatione*. Oxford, Oxford University Press.

Moon, K. (2021), "Aristotle's Disturbing Relatives", *Apeiron* 54: 451–472.

Morales, F. (1994), "Relational Attributes in Aristotle", *Phronesis* 39: 255–274.

Newton, L.A., *John Duns Scotus: Questions on Aristotle's Categories*. Washington (D.C.), The Catholic University of America Press.

Oehler, K. (1984), *Aristoteles: Kategorien*. Berlin, Akademie Verlag.

Owen, G.E.L. (1965), "Inherence", *Phronesis* 10: 97–105.

Palù, C. (2000), "Le definizioni dei relativi nelle *Categorie* di Aristotele: Una risposta a David Sedley", *Dianoia* 5: 39–55.

Pellegrin, P. (2014), *Aristote. Œuvres complètes*. Paris, Flammarion.

Peramatzis, M. (2011), *Priority in Aristotle's Metaphysics*. Oxford, Oxford University Press.

Perinetti, L.A. (1956), "Sulla relazione in Aristotele", *Aut Aut* 33: 236–238.

Philippe, M.D. (1958), "Le relatif dans la philosophie d'Aristote", *Revue des Sciences Philosophiques et Théologiques* 42: 689–710.

Reeve, C.D.C. (2016), *Metaphysics*. Indianapolis, Hackett.

Rini, E. (2010), "L'analisi aristotelica dei relativi", *Rivista di Storia della Filosofia* 65: 623–656.

Rolfe, E. (1995), *Metaphysik*. Darmstadt, Wissenschaftliche Buchgesellschaft.

Ross, W.D. (1924), *Aristotle's Metaphysics. A Revised Text with Introduction and Commentary*, I-II. Oxford, Clarendon Press.

Sachs, J. (1999), *Aristotle's Metaphysics*. Santa Fe (NM), Green Lion Press.

Santos, R. (2016), *Categorias. Da Interpretação*. Lisboa, INCM.

Sedley, D. (2002), "Aristotelian Relativities", *Le style de la pensée: recueil de textes en hommage à Jacques Brunschwig*, ed. M. Canto-Sperber and P. Pellegrin. Paris, Les Belles Lettres: 324–352.

Share, M. (2020), *Philoponus. On Aristotle's Categories 6–15*. London, Bloomsbury Publishing.

Sillitti, G. (1985), "La concezione del *pros ti* e il problema degli enti astratti in Aristotele", *Elenchos* 6: 357–377.

Strange, S.K. (2014), *Porphyry. On Aristotle's Categories*. London, Bloomsbury Publishing.

Thomas Aquinas (1929), *Scriptum super libros Sententiarum*, ed. P. Mandonnet. Paris, P. Lethielleux.

Thomas Aquinas (1981), *The Summa Theologiæ of St. Thomas Aquinas*. Westminster (MD), Christian Classics.

Tredennick, H. (1933), *Metaphysics*, I. Cambridge (MA), Harvard University Press.

Yebra, V.G. (1982), *Metafísica de Aristóteles*. Madrid, Editorial Gredos.

Zanatta, M. (1989), *Aristotele: Le Categorie*. Milano, BUR.

Zucca, D. (2011), "Aristotele, *Categorie* 7, 7b15–8b24: Lo status aporetico dei relative", *Studi sulle Categorie di Aristotele*, ed. M. Bonelli and F. G. Masi. Amsterdam, Adolf M. Hakkert: 191–212.

Index of Passages

Note: Endnotes are indicated by the page number followed by 'n' and the endnote number; e.g., 20n1 refers to endnote 1 on page 20.

Index of Names

Note: Endnotes are indicated by the page number followed by 'n' and the endnote number; e.g., 20n1 refers to endnote 1 on page 20.

For Product Safety Concerns and Information please contact our EU
representative GPSR@taylorandfrancis.com
Taylor & Francis Verlag GmbH, Kaufingerstraße 24, 80331 München, Germany

www.ingramcontent.com/pod-product-compliance
Lightning Source LLC
LaVergne TN
LVHW010938110826
845149LV00013B/2651
* 9 7 8 1 0 3 2 9 1 4 2 8 2 *